DECODING INDIAN BABUDOM

DECODING INDIAN BABUDOM

ASHWINI SHRIVASTAVA

Vitasta
LET KNOWLEDGE SPREAD

Published by
Vitasta Publishing Pvt Ltd
2/15, Ansari Road, Daryaganj
New Delhi-110 002
info@vitastapublishing.com

ISBN 978-93-90961-35-1

First Edition 2022

MRP ₹ 495

Edited by Renu Arya
Cover and layout by Somesh Kumar Mishra
Printed by Vikas Computer and Printers

This book is dedicated to millions of people who wish to see an effective administration. May their wish come true!

Contents

Foreword

I have been watching Ashwini Shrivastava ever since I came into the Ministry of Personnel, Public Grievances and Pensions nearly seven years ago.

I have seen him walking up and down the corridors of North Block. Being a medical clinician, I could easily observe that he was not only compulsively hunting for news but also smelling news.

That itself is the biggest attribute of any budding young journalist who has a passion to make a mark in the field of credible media.

Having been into freelance media writing for several decades, it gives me a huge sense of gratification to see a young journalist seeking to put on record his observations, as noted and analyzed by him over the last ten years while covering the Ministry of Personnel and the Department of Personnel & Training (DoPT) in particular.

Having read the synopsis but not the full text, I cannot endorse or vouchsafe the contents of the book, but I am sure there will be something thought provoking to sit up and take notice of what this young, intelligent friend has to put across.

Ashwini is right when he says that any system of large administration should assiduously work for the betterment of the multitude it serves. That is also the legacy that all those in bureaucracy and public service should leave behind.

This avowed objective has been sought to be achieved to a great extent after Shri Narendra Modi took over as Prime Minister in 2014 and gave us the mantra of 'Maximum Governance Minimum Government' which essentially applies increased transparency, increased citizen participation and zero tolerance against corruption.

The evidence of this is PM Modi's personal intervention to abolish interviews for selection to government jobs and some path-breaking decisions like 'Mission Karmayogi' and National Recruiting Agency (NRA) envisaging a Common Eligibility Test (CET) for job aspirants.

With the world looking up to India as a role model and an inspiration in the aftermath of the COVID-19 pandemic, Ashwini Shrivastava's book may serve as an essential reference manual not only for serving bureaucrats and scholars but also for candidates aspiring to join the civil services and contribute to the making of Modi's New India.

Dr Jitendra Singh

Minister of State (Independent Charge)
Ministry of Science and Technology and Ministry of Earth Sciences
Minister of State in the Prime Minister's Office (PMO)
Ministry of Personnel, Public Grievances and Pensions
Department of Atomic Energy
Department of Space

Message

The Indian Civil Service is an august institution which traces its antecedents back to the British colonial civil service.

In the 75 years of India's independence, the civil service has been praised by many as the vital bond which keeps the country united and running even in the worst of emergencies and is criticized by many for its inefficiency and lack of contact with the grassroots.

Speaking on April 21, 1947, Sardar Patel, the first Home Minister of India, described the creation of the All India Administrative Services as "significant and epoch making".

He said the service will now be free to or will have to adopt its true role of a national service without being trammeled by traditions and habits of the past.

The days when the service could be masters were over and officers must be guided by a real spirit of service in their day-to-day administration.

Referring to a saying that the Indian Civil Service was neither Indian, civil nor imbued with any spirit of service, Sardar Patel declared that it will be the bounden duty of the

Civil Service to treat the common man in India as its own and to feel itself as one of them and amongst them.

The Civil Service will have to learn not to despise or disregard them. He said they should be proud to regard it a privilege to belong to the Civil Service and to uphold throughout their service, its dignity, integrity and incorruptibility.

Civil servants should not approach their tasks from a purely mercenary angle or entirely from self-interest.

The foremost consideration must be how to best contribute to the well being of India as a whole. Service should be rendered without fear or favour and without any expectation of extraneous rewards.

Sardar Patel's words will strike a chord with any Indian. There is no doubt that these lofty ideals are what India deserves from its bureaucracy.

Sadly, the reality has been different.

While much has been achieved in creating a pro-people, pro-development, sensitive and transparent administration, many remain disappointed with what has been delivered by the Civil Service till date.

Reform of the Indian bureaucracy to meet the needs of the 1.3 billion people living in the knowledge society of the 21st century is akin to the impossible task of redesigning an aeroplane while flying.

It is not easy!

However, it is clear that reform of the bureaucracy is a major unfinished task left from the economic liberalization programme of 1991, which completely transformed India in the last three decades.

This book appears at a time when the Government of

India has launched a major reform initiative called 'Mission Karmayogi'. The initiative will be targeting the 4.8 million government employees with a new capacity-building scheme for civil servants aimed at upgrading the post-recruitment training mechanism of the officers and employees at all levels.

This exercise is meant to 'radically' improve the government's human resource management practices and use state-of-the-art infrastructure to augment the capacity of civil servants.

It aims to prepare the Indian civil servants for the future by making them more creative, constructive, imaginative, innovative, proactive, professional, progressive, energetic, enabling, transparent and technology enabled.

It is expected that empowered with specific role-competencies, a civil servant will be able to ensure efficient service delivery of the highest quality standards.

Decoding Indian Babudom by Ashwini Shrivastava is a delightful read.

While there are many books on public administration and bureaucracy written by retired civil servants in the genre of memoirs and reminiscences, there are only a few written by journalists who follow the bureaucracy from the outside.

Thus, this book is a unique non-partisan account by an outsider looking inside the steel frame.

I am happy that Ashwini, whom I know for many years as an outstanding and diligent journalist working for the Press Trust of India, has taken on the arduous task of decoding the Indian bureaucracy through this book.

I am sure it will spur interest and disabuse misconceptions in the minds of the readers about how the bureaucracy works in India.

Despite the massive growth of the private and nonprofit sector in India, the Civil Service remains even today, a most sought after career option.

Our youth vie with each other to enter into the corridors of power. They, in particular, should read this book.

It is commendable that this book was written during Ashwini's spare time – saved from the long commutes to the office and back – during the lockdown necessitated by the COVID-19 restrictions on movement.

I compliment him for making the best productive use of the time saved.

I encourage Ashwini to continue to monitor the changes that are being ushered into the governance of this country and to come out with a sequel to the book with more examples of how the bureaucracy works or does not work.

I strongly recommend this maiden work to all discerning readers. Students, bureaucrats and general readers, especially candidates aspiring to join the civil services, will find the book useful as well as absorbing.

Venu Rajamony

Former Ambassador to the Kingdom of Netherlands
Indian Foreign Service
1986 batch

Preface

Indian bureaucracy is one of the most sought after career options for lakhs of young aspirants who study hard day and night to enter this vivid world of the country's administration through qualifying the toughest civil services examination.

People look at those in bureaucracy as someone with high intellect, hardworking and focused, as these are the main virtues that help them enter this prestigious service.

Bureaucrats draw a great amount of respect from the common man as they are considered to be highly meritorious, knowledgeable and of course influential.

However, there are many challenges that cripple the country's bureaucratic system. To serve a populous country like India is not an easy task, but this cannot be the excuse for an inefficient system.

Most of the times, the common man's grievance fails to reach the higher ups. Those in decision making do not even come to know of the problems faced by the public at the grassroots level.

So, it is desirable that a public servant must have his/her ear towards the general public to understand their problems and subsequently work to solve them.

To serve the people and to get their job done, these public servants need to work at lightning speed.

The casual '*dekhlenge*' (will see to it) attitude from those in government administration frustrates people. A perception of non-cooperation and inefficiency has been attached to the public servants. Government public dealing should be hassle free. People get fed-up with running from pillar to post to get their work done.

In this modern era when people are opting for digital means to ease their life, why is our bureaucracy still tangled in files and paperwork? The ongoing digitization of public work should be implemented in India's bureaucratic system without any delay. This will save time and energy, and make things more systematic.

The common man expects an easy life without much of bureaucratic problems. If they do encounter any difficulty then they also expect a quick solution. This book is an honest attempt to highlight various aspects of the Indian bureaucracy, its ailments and probable solutions. Nowhere does this become a monotonous read as the writer has given full attention in making it easy to read.

It is interesting that as citizens we all can relate to every word written. Many of us have encountered some problems somewhere in getting our work done from government offices like getting certificates from municipal corporations or the District Magistrate's office, getting registration of commercial or personal properties, driving licences, police verification, passport-related work, and what not.

The writer has not only hand-picked the shortcomings of the country's bureaucratic system but at the same time has also presented possible solutions to correct and overcome them. Thus, this book is a complete package in itself.

For the younger generation, who want to make their career in public services, this book is a must-read.

I am sure those in power would also like to go through this book, which can be rightfully termed as a bird's eye view of the country's administrative system by highlighting its different aspects, and pin pointing the scope for improvement.

Last but not the least, the writer has deliberately chosen easy-to-understand words and made to-the-point observations so that the message reaches all in a faster and clearer way.

I have gone through the book and I must admit that it has helped me enhance my understanding of the subject. His 15 sutras (or solutions) for improving the governance has immense potential in bringing about the change that we all aspire to see.

In no way is the book critical of the country's bureaucracy, it is a sincere attempt to highlight the shortcomings and give suggestions to overcome them.

As life partner and colleague, I tried my best to be his constant support in shaping his debut in writing. I wish him the best in life and may this maiden venture inspire him to continue this journey with many more good reads in the future.

Sumedha Shankar
Senior Journalist

Author's Note

The thought of writing this book came to me when I was in Bonn, Germany, in 2018. I was invited as a speaker to share my thoughts on extremism at an event organized by Deutsche Welle media group. I found some of the participants and guest speakers inquisitive about Indian bureaucracy and its tales that had reached them.

The idea couldn't materialize then owing to the hectic schedule that a journalist of a wire agency has. Chasing news and daily filing of stories took priority over this personal desire to author a book.

But the thought kept coaxing me. It was only during the lockdown that I could muster the courage to organize my thoughts and attempt to turn my dream into a reality. While Covid-19 brought miseries to people, it came as a blessing in disguise for me.

Over the course of my decade-and-a-half tryst with bureaucrats, I have met scores of excellent individuals in the labyrinth of Indian bureaucracy. Some were/are very well-known and some not-so-well-known, some very friendly and some standoffish. But each one of them had a story to tell and each one of them had lessons imbibed over years of interaction with the vast population that makes up this land of *'Bharat'*.

India's administrative system is too diverse to be easily understood by an outsider. There are levels of disparities when it comes to ensuring good governance. Vested interests and corruption appear to have set in as the foundation of many government offices.

There is a lack of awareness among people, especially the marginalized, about the working of the bureaucracy. They find governance inaccessible for most of their miseries. Many find the system a maze and a struggle to decipher.

Decoding Indian Babudom is essentially to reveal the generalist and the realistic point of view of the Indian governance system, especially from a common man's perspective.

A governance system where people are treated professionally, irrespective of their social and economic status, and their work is done efficiently is not only desirable but also achievable.

Good governance is a basic right of the citizens of any country. It is the hallmark of a civilized society. Governance is meant to be hassle free, easily accessible and more importantly corruption free.

Its denial erodes people's trust in those who are in power and gives birth to various problems like the monstrous graft and deadly red-tape that ultimately cripples a country.

Constant efforts must be made to ensure good governance. People's needs must be assessed and re-assessed time and again to ensure prompt delivery of services and ease of governance that match their aspirations.

The Indian bureaucratic system is a relic of the past and

one of the few good things which India inherited from the British. It has withstood the test of time and served us well.

While the political masters keep changing, civil servants/ government employees continue to remain part of the very system that runs this huge dynamic country. They are never out of the system thus, making them an inseparable part of governance.

These civil servants are responsible for deciding crucial matters related to 130 crore i.e. 1.3 billion (and growing) people of the country.

There are many tales of this diverse bureaucracy which remain within the framework of the power corridors. While a few get on the wrong path and become news, there are others who work tirelessly, thanklessly and silently for the benefit of the people and ultimately for the country.

Every starry-eyed youngster of my time wanted to get into the Indian Institute of Technology (IIT) or Indian Institute of Management (IIM) or the Civil Services.

On hindsight, I am glad I made the right choice and got into journalism. Here I could get the best of both the worlds – the freedom to write and report about bureaucracy, and the privilege and pleasure of watching bureaucrats at work.

Many civil servants dislike the word '*babu*'. They have similar feelings for the use of the word '*babudom*' and '*babuism*', for reasons best known to them. To me, it doesn't lower their position or image. It is reflective of the perception that largely exists about them outside the '*Babudom*'.

This book is an attempt to highlight what goes inside *Babudom* and some aspects of *Babuism* from the eyes of the common people. It specifically delves into reasons behind the ailments of the country's bureaucratic system and highlights the aspects of the system that are hated by the common man.

I wish to put a disclaimer before the readers start going through this book. Read the ailments and my suggestions to overcome them keeping the common man, who has limited or no access to modern-day governance, in mind.

The book suggests 15 sutras to achieve good governance. These suggestions are based on my experience and threadbare discussions I had with the present and former bureaucrats, subject specialists, journalists and common men.

These suggestions may not be the panacea for improving governance, but there is definitely no harm in trying them.

I have not mentioned big-ticket reforms that may be brought in for the bureaucracy as civil servants and policy makers are capable of doing it, and have been doing it.

I have consciously avoided mentioning the age-old issues of corruption and red-tape in detail. Though, corruption in terms of 'need-based and greed-based graft' is mentioned briefly and discussed at appropriate places in the book.

I have made deliberate efforts not to use jargon and specialized words so that the readers do not have any problem in understanding.

The purpose of this book is not to tell the history or historical facts about the origin of bureaucracy, the origin of Civil Services and its structure in minute detail, for that can be easily done on the internet.

I strongly believe that bureaucracy will have to learn from the past to improve the present and to brighten the future.

The bureaucracy, particularly the officers and all categories of government employees, need to be more conscious of the problems faced by the people on the ground and bring changes – not generalized but specific – to help fellow citizens.

The book tries to highlight the problems being faced by the civil servants/government employees/administration in general besides mentioning some award winning instances of innovation, public service and of putting the country before self.

The book also covers the specific perception attached with bureaucracy and governance in general through answers to ten *Frequently Asked Questions* (FAQs).

I am sure some of the stories of civil servants, honoured with the Prime Minister's award, will inspire lakhs of young aspirants who vie for these coveted posts, year after year.

Youngsters trying to get into government jobs, be it the civil services or at any level, may try and analyze the ailments and perceptions associated with the Indian administrative system highlighted in the book in order to bring in the change.

I am confident about the talent and skills of the civil servants/government employees, both with the central and state governments at all levels, who can bring reforms in the country's governance system.

I, truly, take pride in some of the government employees who leave traditional paths to bring changes in the lives of the common man.

However, the question arises as to why the country's governance system has not yet reached the level where it should be? The book tries to unravel this.

The more I write about the subject, the less it is. I expect readers to draw their own conclusions about the observations and suggestions in the book.

In the process, if I have been able to demystify the visible and invisible ailments related to bureaucracy, I would consider my labour well rewarded and amply justified.

Enjoy reading!

To you, gentle reader, I dedicate this, my maiden foray into the world of book writing.

Sheelam Param Bhushanam
Character, the highest virtue!

BUREAUCRACY without character is akin to a man without one. Character that complements integrity and incorruptibility are expected to be the key traits of any civil servant and all categories of government employees.

Considering the importance of honesty and integrity in the professional and personal conduct of government employees, the phrase *'Sheelam Param Bhushanam'* (character is the highest virtue) is often emphasized.

The phrase is the motto of Lal Bahadur Shastri National Academy of Administration (LBSNAA), Mussoorie – the country's premier institution for imparting training to civil servants.

Due to the ever changing socio economic situation inside and outside the country, it is desired that civil servants be innovative, accountable and efficient while maintaining a sterling character, free from all kinds of allurement.

According to various reports in the media, a number of civil servants, both at the Centre and in State governments, have been victims of harassment and in some cases intimidation, for holding on to the virtue of '*sheelam*' while carrying out their professional duty.

There have been umpteen instances of corruption in the public domain involving government officials. Most of the times, the scale of corruption not only surprises the country but makes people worry.

While a high degree of character is desirable in government employees, there have been instances where this must-have quality gets compromised owing to various internal and external factors.

One may blame individual greed or collapse of institutional structures created by the founding fathers of bureaucracy, as reasons for officers/staff found lacking in character. However, it is an individual's failure in keeping up with the ethos of the ethical work force.

To have an administrative structure that is manned by honest and efficient employees/civil servants, it is essential that they are protected from allurements of corruption from the outside world.

Possessing high character can yield efficient, innovative and courageous thinking from a civil servant/government employee by protecting them from the ills of corruption.

But what makes government employees susceptible to fall for greed or become inefficient? One of the reasons for the malaise is explained in the chapter titled – 'Yeh Dil Maange Mor'...Need, greed or accepted norm?'

The power that these civil servants enjoy and exercise is immense.

Imagine a young bureaucrat who has been posted as the Collector-cum-District Magistrate (DM) in a district! He is all-in-all of the district under him. Many feel that this power slowly and steadily goes into the bureaucrat's persona.

There are government employees, who may not be senior officials but working at crucial posts of clerks or any other mid-level executive role, who too are involved in corruption.

There is no denying the fact that a government job gives an individual a social status, financial security and makes him feel privileged.

While most respect all these, there are a few who misuse it thus, getting a label of being snobbish or a *'sahab'* (meaning boss) from the common man.

It is not only civil servants who may be solely blamed for the condition of governance that we see today. There are other categories of government employees too, be it peons, clerks and middle level executives, who are part of the problem.

To have an effective bureaucracy that is sensitive towards people and of the needs and aspirations of the country, it ought to have character.

A character that is marked by empathy and values of honesty, integrity, hard work and willingness to work without prejudice for all sections of the society with all their might!

Without this strength of character, bureaucrats would continue to fail in showing the much-needed commitment to the country and fellow citizens.

This quality is needed more in middle and low level staff. The ones who are not officers but part of the typical government system involved in processing a work from scratch – proposing to put up a file, not to approve it or getting it approved.

To sum up, one may not agree more with Sardar Patel's address to the All India Service probationers on 21 April

1947, where he had said, "A civil servant cannot afford to and must not take part in politics. Nor must he involve himself in communal wrangles. To depart from the path of rectitude in either of these respects is to debase public service and to lower its dignity."

Truer words on the subject have never been spoken.

Hum Aapke Hai Kaun?
Perpetual saga of trust deficit!

YOU hardly come across a large number of people praising the country's bureaucracy or administrative system. You may call it their bias or lack of awareness but their perception is not far from reality.

There is a strong perception about bureaucracy that it is by nature corrupt, besides being snobbish and procrastinating.

The main reason behind such perceptions is that sincere attempts have not been made by civil servants or those in government service to get rid of these 'labels'.

I do not need to narrate details of all the good work being done by civil servants, despite political and administrative constraints, for the welfare of masses.

Some of the good works carried out by them are highlighted in the latter part of the book.

The intention behind raking up this existing phenomenon is to bring it to the notice of the people and civil servants that this perception is still very much prevalent even today, almost three-quarters of a century after the country's independence.

I have had the privilege of traveling widely across the length and breadth of this great country, and to some places abroad, due to my work commitments as a journalist and for my love for the same.

My profession has also given me ample opportunity to interact with people I met during the course of fulfilling my professional duties or following my personal hobby of traveling.

I have been taking feedback on different matters, including bureaucracy and governance, from people in rural as well as in urban areas.

These people, who I have interacted with in the course of my professional work, are tea stall owners/workers, farmers, small shopkeepers, drivers and labourers, among others.

I can safely vouch that I speak most people's mind to say that majority of citizens are not happy with the way the country's governance works.

One may ignore the always discontented lot but the views of the majority need to be considered.

In fact, the majority feels that governance is meant for rich people and the poor man's words and problems do not reach the ears of those in the corridors of power.

This widespread perception of inefficiency and corruption is the result of some callous government employees. This ultimately tarnishes the image of bureaucracy inside and outside the country.

It is believed that there has to be less of government and more of good governance – maximum governance and minimum government – and that the common people should not face any problem in dealing with government employees, either in terms of corruption or bad behaviour.

That is an ideal system of governance which sadly still

eludes the masses despite all the advancements and tall claims made by the government.

We do hear cases of harassment, corruption and red-tape from common people who approach government offices for different works.

The country is relying on digitization of the government's work. While considerable progress has been achieved by most of the central government departments and a few state governments, but there still exists a long road ahead to convert it into reality.

But there is a road! And this road needs to be followed for the destination to be fast achieved.

The efforts by the Ministry of Personnel, Public Grievances and Pensions in bringing in e-office or electronic office in central government organizations are praiseworthy.

Some of the state governments have done or are doing a commendable job in digitizing public service related work.

However, I still fail to fathom why the governments (central and states) have not yet achieved 100 per cent digitization of government work, given that India is a leading power in technology.

At least, the working of departments dealing with public service, especially in the states/union territories must be digitized completely and quickly to keep corruption and red-tape at bay.

I must also praise Aadhaar (a 12-digit unique identification number issued by the Unique Identification Authority of India or UIDAI) and other digital initiatives by the central and state governments to check corruption. They are well-envisaged and have been bringing in the desired results as well.

It is still a mystery that why a decision (like digitization of government's work or the ones related to public service delivery in states/UTs) taken by a bureaucrat, that needs to be implemented by his/her senior or junior colleagues – most possibly from the same service, i.e. the Indian Administrative Service (IAS) – moves at a pace that doesn't match people's aspirations.

I also say this in reference to all the welfare measures and technological changes that are being brought in by the government for the welfare of the masses and to improve the efficiency of bureaucracy.

The world is not going to stand still for us or to allow us to reach their level of digitized governance!

For this, we need to buckle up.

There are many examples of good governance measures being practiced globally. Look at our not-so-distant neighbour Singapore.

Almost every year, perhaps excluding the coronavirus pandemic period that barred people's movement, some of our civil servants go to Singapore to pursue a course in administration or good governance at the prestigious Lee Kuan Yew School of Public Policy.

I was in Singapore in 2019 for a journalism fellowship. I must say that the school is world-class and imparts the best knowledge.

The school has been named after the founder and the first Prime Minister of Singapore, Lee Kuan Yew or LKY, known for his out-of-box thinking that made Singapore into what it is today.

How LKY transformed the state of affairs in Singapore is a fact and all in public governance know and must try to pursue in letter and spirit in India.

Our bureaucrats go world over to upgrade their knowledge and sharpen their skills.

But then why are we still lacking in delivering the governance that most of the people of this country need or desire? Its causes are clearly in the realm of self-introspection for all concerned.

I have personally experienced that the government machinery works at lightning speed if it wants something to be done. But why does this conviction take a back-seat when it comes to implementing most of the pro-people related work. It is beyond my comprehension.

Civil servants and all categories of government employees may bear in mind that people of this country aspire for results and not promises. Conscious efforts are needed to bridge this trust deficit between people and the government.

Its continuous failure will simply erode people's trust and take away their confidence from the government, and ultimately from the civil servants and the *babus*.

How hard is it for a government employee to work efficiently and in a manner expected from him without any expectation or gratification?

A B C of Bureaucracy...

Bureaucracy is the backbone of the governance system of a country without which no government can function effectively.

The functioning of the Government of India is structured with the President of India at the top as the executive head, followed by the Prime Minister (who is the head of council of ministers), then the council of ministers including the cabinet ministers, ministers of state and deputy ministers, and then the executives – secretaries and subordinate functionaries.

As the country is a union of states and union territories, there is a resembling structure for them.

In case of states, the Governor is at the top, followed by the Chief Minister of the State, (who also heads the council of ministers), then the council of ministers including the cabinet ministers and ministers of state, and then the executive – starting with the Chief Secretary (who is the top bureaucrat of the state) and subordinate functionaries.

In case of Union Territories, there is a Lieutenant Governor, supported by the executive 'and then' the typical bureaucratic set up. In some union territories or set of union territories there is an administrator too to take care of governance.

Indian government employees can be divided into three broad categories: Group A, Group B and Group C (Group D that comprised support staff has been merged with Group C at the centre level). Some states also follow this three-tier structure.

The top group consists of two types of services – All India Services and the Group A Civil Services at the Centre. In states, there are officers from State Civil Services that are part of the top tier of the bureaucracy.

All India Services

Many read about this term - 'All India Services', but some still have difficulty in understanding it.

India has at present three All India Services – Indian Administrative Service (IAS), Indian Police Service (IPS) and Indian Forest Service (IFoS).

Its members are posted in central government departments or in states, which are also known as cadre state.

A cadre is a state or a group of states/union territories that the members of these three All India Services are allocated.

History lessons

The All India Services Act of 1951 had specifically defined two services – the IAS and the IPS, as the All India Services. However, the same law has provision to create three more services under this category – the IFoS, the Indian Medical and Health Service (IMHS) and the Indian Service of Engineers (irrigation, power, buildings and roads).

Barring the IFoS, the other two services could not be constituted owing to reasons best known to the policy makers. There exists the Indian Engineering Service (IES), though it is not an All India Service.

Article 312 of the Constitution of India has provisions related to the All India services. It says "…Parliament may, by law, provide for the creation of one or more All India Services (including an All-India Judicial Service) common to the Union and the States, and subject to other provisions of this Chapter, regulate the recruitment, and the conditions of service of persons appointed, to any such service".

(The Constitution of India was adopted on January 26, 1950)

The All India Judicial Service could not be created. In 2020, the government decided to set up this service to recruit officers for subordinate courts through an entrance test.

Coming back to the All India Services, officers of these services are common to the centre and states and can be posted anywhere in the Union of India.

One of the purposes behind creating these All India Services was to maintain the spirit of 'unity in diversity' as officers of one state can get posted to central government departments or go to other cadres/states.

Besides these three All India Services, the rest including the Indian Foreign Service (IFS), Indian Revenue Service (Income-Tax), Indian Revenue Service (Customs and Central Excise) and Indian Information Service (IIS), among others are included in Group A services.

Among them all, the IAS is arguably the most sought-after and the most influential service of the country. These men and women literally run this country's bureaucratic governance. Literally!

Then, you have the Indian Foreign Service, the diplomats, to manage the country's foreign affairs and related matters.

The Indian Police Service (IPS) manages law and order in the country besides intelligence collection and dissemination.

The Indian Forest Service deals with management of the country's flora and fauna. In a country like India, with a significant green cover and abundant natural resources, it is an important job.

Similarly, you have the Indian Revenue Service (customs and central excise) to look after work related to the collection of indirect taxes, its management and handling of evasion, among others. There is also Indian Revenue Service (Income Tax). As the nomenclature suggests, its members look after work related to the collection of direct taxes, among others.

So, in a nutshell, there are specialized services to manage almost all departments of the government essential to run the country.

For instance, India has eight Group A services exclusively to run the Indian railways. Some of these include the exclusive Indian Railway Service of Engineers (IRSE), Indian Railway Traffic Service (IRTS), Indian Railway Service of Mechanical

Engineers (IRSME) and Indian Railway Personnel Service (IRPS), among others.

However, the government in March 2020 decided to merge all of them to form the Indian Railway Management Service to end multi-layered departmentalism and to make the outfit run as one cohesive unit.

That said, it does not mean that officers of these Group A services run this huge country and its infrastructure entirely on their own.

To execute and process them, they have a key Group B and Group C cadre or categories respectively.

The Group B posts in India are manned by senior level functionaries in the mid-tier of bureaucracy. They consist of Section Officers and Assistant Section Officers. They manage a particular section of the government department.

And lastly, Group C which consists of all the clerical and support staff.

Mind you, the most common perception about the Indian bureaucracy in the minds of the common man is based on the experience they get after interacting with Group B and C employees for their work.

Not many people are fortunate enough to meet senior officers, bypassing their subordinates, for official work. There appears to be an unwritten principle of strictly regulating the common man's entry to government departments to meet senior officers or the head of the departments.

I am aware of the provision of 'public meeting day' by the officers to meet people who may have grievances. But ask anyone how difficult it is? It is more honoured in the breach than in the observance.

There may be some who are able to meet a senior officer in a government office in case of work but more certainly needs to be done.

People should have hassle free access to the concerned government officials to raise their grievances. Such grievances need to be responded to swiftly and in a time-bound manner.

State governments can especially further strengthen online grievance redressals, close on the lines of the central government departments.

The Centralized Public Grievance Redress and Monitoring System (CPGRAMS) – an online system that allows people to raise a complaint mainly against central government departments – by the Union Ministry of Personnel, Public Grievances and Pensions is a praiseworthy step.

A separate work flow and functionality for grievances to appeal to the authorities in CPGRAMS has been operationalized.

The timeline for resolution of an appeal by the nodal appellate authority is 30 days of receipt of the same.

A Parliamentary Committee has in its report tabled in Parliament on March 16, 2021, said that the poor and marginalized should be able to reap the benefits of CPGRAMS.

"For this to happen, there should be a mechanism in place to take note of grievances involving larger public interest featuring in newspapers.

"The Committee is happy to note that the Department has already taken an initiative in this regard. The Committee recommends the Department to impress upon ministries/departments of the central government to set up such mechanism at the earliest and monitor the action taken by them," the Department-Related Parliamentary Standing Committee on Personnel, Public Grievances, Law and Justice said in its 106th report on Demands for Grants (2021-22) of the Ministry of Personnel, Public Grievances and Pensions.

Concentrated efforts can be put in place to ensure that states also adopt such measures using a common platform and that the resolution is time-bound. There is a need to make CPGRAMS available in other main regional languages as well.

Coming back to the structure of the Indian administrative system, the work flow is divided into two main components:

1. Affairs related to the Union of India
2. Affairs related to the states/union territories

There are about 48.34 lakh (4.8 million) central government employees as on March 13, 2020, as per an official data[1]. The state governments are said to have an estimated two crore plus (20 million) employees.

According to the Sixth Economic Census (2013), around 131.29 million persons were employed in 58.5 million establishments.

Out of the 131.29 million persons, 7.2 per cent of workers were employed in government or public sector undertakings.

As per the census, the growth rate of employment since 2005 was 38.13 per cent.

Selection of civil servants

The Union Public Service Commission (UPSC), a New Delhi-based constitutional body, is responsible for selecting civil servants for the country.

---

1 https://pib.gov.in/PressReleaseIframePage.aspx?PRID=1606285

It also does selection for certain Group B posts.

Then there are other recruitment agencies like the Staff Selection Commission (SSC) – that is mandated to make recruitment to Group 'B' (non-Gazette) and Group 'C' (non-technical) posts in various ministries/departments of the Government of India and their attached and subordinate offices.

Similarly, state governments have their own recruitment process to select their officers and subordinate staff.

Certain central and state government owned organizations have also been vested with the power to do their own recruitments.

The rules relating to service and superannuation may vary from state to state, fine-tuned to local requirements and conditions.

In 2020, the central government decided to have a computer-based Common Eligibility Test (CET) for recruitment to non-gazette posts. This test will be conducted by the National Recruitment Agency (NRA). It is a welcome step, as of now.

If you look broadly, the governance structure or the role of bureaucracy is well-defined and the rules made by them to run the country are people-friendly.

Despite that, gaps remain in having an effective and people-friendly governance system.

Kaam Kaise Hota Hai?

How does bureaucracy function?

THE country's administrative system works through a nearly six-decade old set of rules, though parts of these rules are periodically modified.

There are two crucial rules – The Government of India (Allocation of Business) Rules, 1961 and The Government of India (Transaction of Business) Rules, 1961[2].

I am one of the strongest advocates, though in minority, demanding complete redrafting (if not overhauling) of these rules to match governance-related needs of the country and its people in future.

The Government of India (Allocation of Business) Rules, 1961 allocates work broadly among its different offices – ministries, departments and subordinate departments/organizations.

The Government of India (Transaction of Business) Rules, 1961, has defined the processes and responsibilities for disposing the government business or works.

2 Both these important rules can be accessed at the Cabinet Secretariat website, i.e. www.cabsec.gov.in

The working of the central government is divided into different ministries/departments. There are subordinate offices, attached offices, constitutional and statutory bodies, autonomous bodies and public sector undertakings.

A typical set-up in a Government of India's department has a Secretary as the head of the department, supervising and guiding all its activities.

The Secretary, a high-ranking officer, is assisted by officers at the levels of Special Secretary, Additional Secretary, Joint Secretary, Director, Deputy Secretary and Under-Secretary.

Below that level, the hierarchy of other category of staff starts. These are Section Officers, Assistant Section Officers and the clerical staff. There is a similar system of hierarchy in the administration of state governments and union territories.

There are officers like Revenue Officers (better known as *Tehsildars*), Sub-Divisional Magistrates (SDMs), Additional District Magistrates (ADMs) and District Magistrates (DMs) to look after different administrative work in rural and urban areas.

At the district level, there exists a mechanism known as *'Zila'* (meaning district) *Panchayat* – an elected body of representatives – and *Panchayat* (usually five people selected by locals to look after or coordinate with the government authorities relating to various affairs of a village) to cater to the needs of rural areas.

A typical workflow is explained through the following flow chart:

Movement of files

From Dealing Hand to Section Officer, Under Secretary/Branch Officer, Divisional Head (Deputy Secretary/Director), Joint

Secretary/Additional Secretary/Special Secretary, Secretary and then to the Minister and the Prime Minister as the case may be.

Workflow Chart

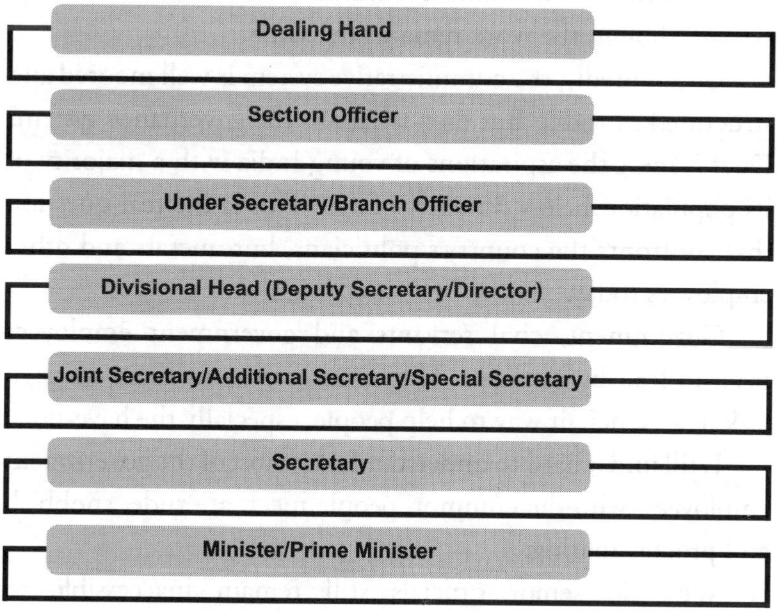

(Source: Central Secretariat Manual of Office Procedure prepared by the Ministry of Personnel, Public Grievances and Pensions.)

The aforesaid flowchart is mainly for disposing routine work related to people.

All work need not go to the top level as there are well defined hierarchy/level of officers for disposal of a work or for decision making.

For majority of policy decisions, a typical administrative structure in the government follows a top-down approach. Political master or policy makers are at the top echelon of a pyramid-like structure that take a policy decision and ensure its implementation by the civil servants and all levels of secretariat and field staff.

In a multi-culture country like India, it is said that language changes every 50-100 km. It is similar with the administrative system, though the work remains the same.

Undoubtedly, the administrative system is well moored and structured in India. But then what ails the governance system? Does it meet the aspirations of young India with a majority of its population below 35 years of age? This is the real question that confronts the country's politicians, bureaucrats and other employees today.

Government, civil servants and government employees need to lead by example. They must carry out their assigned task in an efficient way to help people, especially the have-nots.

I still find it hard to understand why most of the government employees, who the common people meet, are rude, snobbish and procrastinating.

Why do senior officials still remain inaccessible to the common man? Why cannot technology and Artificial Intelligence be used more to ensure ease of governance?

Instead of answering these questions I hope the government employees set themselves as examples of an efficient workforce.

Yeh Dil Maange More...
Corruption: Need, greed or accepted norm?

"BEHIND every successful fortune, there is a crime" is the famous dialogue from the cult American movie Godfather.

Corruption is a widespread problem which has worryingly engulfed the country's bureaucratic system. This monster has not even spared the private sector. They too suffer from it.

For the sake of explanation, corruption in the public sector can be divided into three broad categories – 'need-based', 'greed-based' and 'accepted'.

The third is the most dangerous of all. There is a thin line in these three distinctions of this social evil.

Let me first talk about the most common one – the need-based corruption. It acts as a stepping stone for most of the young civil servants or government employees, who are mainly from humble background and have toiled hard to be part of the civil services or the country's bureaucracy/administrative system and who experience it usually in their first posting.

Did you think this is not possible and words like morality comes to your mind? Think again and this problem may then perhaps stand tall in front of you.

Coming from a humble background could mean being the lone earner of the family. The situation gets tough after marriage or with additional family responsibility. This is coupled with concerns over maintaining themselves as officers or government employees.

There are instances of corruption in the recruitment for government jobs too. Admitting that it exists, an individual getting into the government services using this avoidable route needs to pay back as well!

I feel that public servants and government employees in the country are not well paid which may be one of the principal reasons for corruption.

It requires a great character for an out-of-the-academy bureaucrat and a new recruit in the government to resist small favours and then not get into the vicious cycle of quid-pro-quo.

Many would say that they should control and continue to uphold the value expected from them. It is easier said than done, though.

This is the need-based corruption that can grow like a Godzilla if not nipped in the bud.

If needs are not taken care of by the government by providing sufficient pay and perks to civil servants/government employees from the early stages of their careers, then they become more susceptible to this need-based corruption cycle.

I could not agree more when some anti-corruption experts use the word 'born corrupt' for some government employees. Providing any amount of sufficient pay and perks may not satiate their urge to get more.

From time to time the government considers raising the salary of its employees to ensure that they do not stray on to corrupt paths and their needs are well-taken care of.

I, however, differ with the pay panel's rationale or official claim that the civil servants/employees are well paid.

There are many discrepancies in pay structures besides charges of favouritism towards two services – Indian Administrative Service (IAS) and Indian Foreign Service (IFS), while deciding on raising salaries and allowances by the government appointed Central Pay Commission, usually once in every ten years.

Background on Pay Panel

A Central Pay Commission (CPC) is set up by the Government of India to recommend changes in an employee's pay, allowances and other facilities/benefits, in cash or kind. It gives its reports periodically, usually once in ten years.

The seventh pay commission's report was submitted to the government on November 19, 2015 while its recommendations came into force from January 1, 2016.

While the central government agreed to most of its recommendations for its employees, some of the state governments have not adhered to them in toto.

Continuing on the pay panel, the government makes conscious efforts by accepting the recommendations of the CPC to attract talent to its workforce.

But the money the government gives to a young civil servant, who joins the service, is most of the times less than the salary earned by his probable contemporaries passed out from some premier institutes such as the Indian Institutes of Management (IIMs), Indian Institutes of Technology (IITs) and working in multi national companies (MNCs).

Reiterating: Paying handsome salary to civil servants may be a big deterrent to check corruption. But it also needs to be ensured that they deliver.

Talking about the greed-based corruption, I feel it is all-pervading among the new-age bureaucrats – the millennials getting into the coveted services or into government jobs.

So, how to check this greed-based corruption?

No, we do not need any new rules or laws. We already have far too many. We just need to ensure that the corrupt are punished swiftly and strictly. Fear of law and swift punishment to the guilty always acts as a strong deterrence against any crime. Also, preventive vigilance is better than punitive vigilance.

Lastly, there is this accepted form of corruption. There are certain departments and some government works where (some) people are supposed to give money even if it is not asked in as many words.

Readers would agree that sometime one has to pay a token amount to a policeman's visit for doing credentials check or address verification for the purpose of getting a government job or passport.

If one tries to be honest by avoiding to 'pay' then he or she should be ready for an elongated process.

This is the most common experience which almost all applicants must have gone through with the police personnel doing passport verification.

This is not the end of the saga. Here is a double whammy. Those who have paid the police personnel to write the factual report (which they are expected to do without taking bribe) also have to cough up money to get the passport from the postman.

Please note, there are exceptions and many policemen/

postmen have a great character. I am referring to those handful of them who at times defame the department by extorting convenience fee for carrying out their official work, for which they are already being paid a salary from the taxpayers' money.

I still wonder why such work of doing verification cannot be digitized completely!

The experience of people at municipal corporations for getting life/death certificates and while getting a job done in offices like development authorities and housing boards is the same. No money, no work!

Today, people also do not have the time to invest in frequent follow-ups with government officials, needless to say unsupportive, if they refuse to pay them the convenience fee.

Sad but true, there exists an organized corruption in most of the government departments/organizations and it goes on right under the sun.

To perceive that the entire bureaucracy/government administrative system is corrupt would be gross injustice to the bulk of the honest and dedicated civil servants and government employees.

A broad brush should not be used to paint all of them as corrupt though there are some bad eggs and black sheep like in all professions.

Corruption undoubtedly plagues the country, its citizens, especially the downtrodden ones, and erodes people's trust in the governance system.

There is strong evidence and many instances to determine that institutional corruption does exist in many of the government departments. The situation is comparatively grim in the departments controlled by the state governments.

The existence of corruption across the length and breadth of our vast country dents our image at the international level and makes India a less preferred destination for investment which, in turn, can add to deficiency in jobs and employment opportunities.

The Government of India has a zero tolerance policy towards corruption but the euphemistically termed 'speed money' is still making its move in the country's administrative system.

India has been ranked at an unenviable 86th position among 180 countries and territories in the Corruption Perception Index (CPI) prepared by Transparency Watchdog and released in January 2021.

One can safely assume the ample scope for improvement for the country in the index.

India has also ratified the United Nations Convention Against Corruption (UNCAC), a multilateral international treaty, to strengthen its fight against graft.

So, do we lack anti-corruption laws or organizations to check graft domestically? The answer is a categorical 'No'. There are rules and laws in the country with enough teeth for the governments to punish the guilty.

We have Prevention of Corruption Act of 1988, the anti-corruption law which was amended most recently in 2018, to bring within its ambit the bribe givers too, for the first time. Those who accept bribe were already punishable under the 1988 law. The amended Act has also brought commercial organizations into its ambit besides provisions for punishing the bribe givers too.

The country has the institution of *Lokpal,* the anti-corruption ombudsman, which was set up in 2019 to inquire and investigate allegations of corruption against public functionaries including the Prime Minister of India.

India has the Central Vigilance Commission (CVC), the country's probity watchdog; Central Bureau of Investigation (CBI), the federal agency to probe corruption and other serious crimes; the Income Tax Department and the Enforcement Directorate, to name a few.

There exists a plethora of organizations and sufficient laws to check corruption. Besides, there are provisions in relevant laws to confiscate properties acquired through ill-gotten wealth by corrupt people.

But then, why do we still suffer from this dreaded disease of corruption?

The answer is lack of political and administrative will!

There is no end to human greed. As it is said there is enough for everyone's need but not for everyone's greed.

Based on my interaction with experts and personal experience, the best way to deal with corruption is swift and strictest action against the corrupt to instill the fear of law of the land among them!

This fear can be a great deterrent to check corruption.

A timely completion of probe and time-bound, real time-bound, disposal of corruption cases by all levels of judiciary would add immensely in checking corruption in the country.

My lord, Mercy!

Free and unhindered journalism, use of the transparency laws (like the Right to Information or RTI Act, 2005) and digitization of government works especially that require public dealing, will be the panacea to check corruption and bring more transparency in governance.

In March 2021, a parliamentary committee had asked the transparency watchdog Central Information Commission (CIC) to spread awareness about the RTI Act in rural areas.

The panel expressed concern over a large number of vacancies in the posts of Information Commissioners in State Information Commissions and asked the CIC to furnish a status note in three months.

"The Committee is of the view that rural masses, the people most vulnerable to corrupt practices, are the ones who know the least about their rights under the RTI Act," the Department Related Parliamentary Standing Committee on Personnel, Public Grievances, Law and Justice said in its 106th report on Demands for Grants (2021-22) of the Ministry of Personnel, Public Grievances and Pensions.

The Parliamentary Committee report has been highlighted to impress on the importance of transparency in governance and for the proper implementation of the RTI Act.

Any reform in the Indian bureaucracy would be insufficient without talking about measures to stem corruption.

I feel the issue of corruption is like corona in the Indian context. We want to get over it, vaccination is also available to contain it, but people are avoiding vaccine and allowing the dreaded corona-like virus of corruption to communicate and affect us all.

Frequently Asked Questions

IN an effort to ensure that the book doesn't become a monotonous read I tried to break the monotony by introducing a question and answer format to talk about different aspects of *Babudom*.

In this chapter, I have answered ten *Frequently Asked Questions (FAQs)* on the country's bureaucracy and its working.

There are questions on civil servants/government employees' efficiency and perceptions about the Indian governance system, coaxing the people of the country.

People wonder why the country's public sector is riddled with inefficiency, graft, red-tape and at times insensitive approach.

Government employees, including civil servants, are public servants. They are mandated to carry out tasks to serve the people and ultimately the country. However, there are instances that show the opposite. Based on the feedback from a select group of social and anti-corruption activists, serving and retired bureaucrats, and of course a large number of common men, here are some frequently asked questions that I have tried to answer.

Is privatisation a solution to check corruption?

Corruption is neither limited nor exclusive to government employees/organizations. It is more of a personal trait than an institutional one.

There have been attempts to privatize some of the government entities and work allocated to them more for want of better services and ease in their management but less for checking corruption.

The government can hire private sector specialists to check corruption. For instance, the central government has initiated the process of privatizing its debt-ridden flag carrier Air India.

It has also decided to allow the private sector to run trains on select routes with some conditions, making the first such attempt in over 167 years of the history of Indian railways, which is a behemoth.

The Ministry of External Affairs has taken the help of a private firm in processing applications for passports. It has proven to be a successful and seamless experience drawing appreciation from users/applicants.

The government is making attempts. However, these attempts at times attract a reverse force from within. Its very own bureaucrats who want to ensure their monopoly over government services and in managing governance so that they continue to prosper. These statusquoists are the bane of the whole system.

I do not feel that the entire government services need to be privatized. Instead, to ensure better services, the existing workforce can be motivated, trained, skilled and groomed to be more professional in serving the people and the country.

However, a well-thought out approach and strategy is

needed to allow private sector specialists in select areas of government. Their entry in most areas of governance appears imminent though and could be a welcome step.

The Government of India and some state governments have been encouraging development work on the basis of public private partnership.

It is a good step forward and needs to be emulated by all central and state government departments. However, the big challenge would be to keep at bay the typical red-tape and corruption from affecting such partnerships.

India can take a leaf from other developed countries including Singapore, in running an effective administrative network and governance system where talent is appreciated, bona fide mistakes are ignored and equal career prospects for growth are provided to civil servants.

The recruitment of private sector specialists in government, which is known as lateral entry in official parlance, has already started.

The central government had in 2018 invited applications from eligible candidates for ten posts of joint secretaries in ten different departments. Usually, the post of Joint Secretary is manned by a senior civil servant selected through the civil services examination conducted by UPSC.

A total of 6,077 applications were received by the government. Of these, 64 were called for interview and eight of them were finally appointed in 2019.

Out of these, seven are in position (as on March 2021). The government has also proposed to fill three posts at the Joint Secretary level through lateral entry mode.

The government has maintained there has been no adverse

impact on the morale of the civil servants recruited through the three-stage rigorous civil services examination process.

However, a section of bureaucracy has been strongly opposing such recruitments, both officially and unofficially and in their own typical discreet way.

The government has announced that it would induct 40 more private sector specialists – 27 at the level of Director and 13 at Deputy Secretary level, in its different organizations.

The government has been doing its bit to constantly revive the administration. It is for the bureaucracy to decide on its course correction – whether it would be open to mend its ways or prepare to embrace parachuted colleagues from the private sector.

In a nutshell, the experiment of bringing in private sector specialists is underway and whether they would prove to be an asset, free from corruption, is something only time will tell.

The call for privatization by the government may also wake up from deep slumber some slack bureaucrats/government employees and they may hopefully become productive assets.

What is the solution to end red-tape?

Red-tapism and corruption are interconnected and quite frustrating for citizens and businessmen. The red-tape is real and it exists in some form or the other in all government departments. It is one of the reasons behind the reputation/notoriety of bureaucracy today!

It can be experienced very easily in civic bodies and departments like land, revenue, police and hospital etc, dealing with common people for their official work. This is often a pretext for corruption and in some other cases an instrument of dilatory tactics.

However, if some palms are not greased, red-tapism can stall big investment proposals from businessmen or even a trivial and routine job. It appears that some employees do not take interest in doing what they are paid to do unless there is gratification.

Lackadaisical approach by the employees, often by those holding clerical posts, in helping citizens with their work, ill treatment of those not well-versed in getting their work done and dilatory tactics is a normal scene witnessed in many a government department.

It is not that red-tapism has rendered our bureaucracy ineffective but there is big, BIG, scope for improvement. This can eventually lead to increase in productivity of the government's work and greater people satisfaction.

Most of us have read about and listened to the country's former Defence Minister (Late) George Fernandes' description related to red-tapism.

He had reportedly referred to a bureaucratic orbit where official files are said to be kept in constant movement with the intention of keeping its disposal pending.

Irked over delay in processing one such file, Mr Fernandes had reportedly once sent two senior bureaucrats, then working in his ministry, to Siachen in Jammu and Kashmir when he came to know that they 'sat over' them.

Fernandes became the Defence Minister on March 19, 1998 but had to quit the post following a scandal. He returned as the Defence Minister in October 2001 after his name was cleared in that scandal and he continued in the post till May 2, 2004.

Fernandes, a rare reformist leader, breathed his last on

January 29, 2019 after a prolonged illness.

Coming back to red-tapism, it is very sad to notice people making frequent visits to a government department for their routine work, which should be done promptly. Instead, they are made to run from pillar to post and suffer unnecessary hardship thanks to the ubiquitous red-tape.

One doesn't need to apply rocket science to end red-tapism. It requires scrupulous and sincere supervisory officers at all levels to be more vigilant about their subordinates. Most work, if digitized, can help in ending this malaise. No, we don't need any new rule or law. We already have some that set timelines for doing a job. It is less of rule and more of strict surveillance and courage to reform a system.

If a government department's head, usually a senior officer of the IAS, decides to end red-tapism from his or her department, no power in the world can stop him. Did somebody whisper corruption?

Why could our bureaucracy not manage the exodus of migrants' during the national lockdown in 2020?

India's administrative structure typically works at three crucial levels, PM, CM and DM – Prime Minister, Chief Minister and District Magistrate. While the PM and CM are political appointees, a DM is a bureaucrat, usually an IAS officer or an officer of the state civil services.

The country, like the rest of the world, faced the pandemic, an unprecedented crisis of unimaginable magnitude in the form of coronavirus. Though the early lockdown announced by the Prime Minister on March 24, 2020 helped in checking the spread of the deadly virus, it was bound to cause some hardship to people. The poor, as always the most vulnerable in the case of any calamity, were badly hit.

Who doesn't remember the picture of a woman pulling a briefcase, with all the family's belongings, while walking on the road (perhaps, on way to her native place) using cloth as a string and her son sleeping on it. It was heart-rending for all of us.

Remember, the teenage girl who reportedly cycled from Gurugram in Haryana to Darbhanga in Bihar, covering around 1,200 km on road with her father as a pillion rider.

And the unfortunate death of 16 labourers, all of whom were run over by a goods train in Maharashtra's Aurangabad.

No words can describe the hardships that were faced by many during the lockdown.

There are many such tales of migrant labourers and their family members. Poor people were hit hard by the lockdown woes.

The government's preventive measures to check the coronavirus resulted in mass movement of daily wage workers who were employed in industrial units, commercial outlets or were doing other jobs in the construction sector.

Some people, including women and kids, came out on the road braving the harsh sun in search of public or private transport to reach their home towns.

The government had shut down workplaces and banned public transport as part of the nation wide measures to reduce the spread of the virus.

The movement of these migrant labourers in some instance was also a panic reaction that was fast gripping this unorganized working class, which forms the backbone of the commercial and industrial establishments.

A may blame B! It may be a political or an administrative failure or sheer mismanagement by those in power who could have managed the situation better. Finger pointing serves no purpose though.

A collector or a District Magistrate is incharge of a district. It was his or her primary responsibility, in close consultation and coordination with the Superintendent of Police (SP) or the concerned police officer, to manage the crowd and ensure that nobody faces any problem or gets affected by the virus.

There were some DMs who did manage well. However, there certainly appears to be complete chaos in the administrative set-up, may be due to the unexpected magnitude of the problem.

The exodus of people in some areas is dubbed as a collective failure of the governance machinery including those in power. We, the people, can also not be spared from shouldering this responsibility. The sad truth is that much more could have been done to mitigate the suffering of the migrant labourers who trudged hundreds of miles to reach their homes.

The entire administration appeared to have been caught off guard in managing the large movement of the people. This can be considered an excuse by many, especially when the mandate given to the administrator was to look after the welfare of the citizens.

Do frequent transfers and postings act as means of corruption for those in power?

Relevant service rules allow governments to transfer and post government employees to any departments under them in 'public interest' or due to administrative exigencies.

Dig deeper and one would realize how often this 'public

interest' pretext is misused for vested interest. I do not need to tell you about state governments who have said to have set 'rates' for transfers and postings.

Every time there is a change of government at the centre or in the states, an unending saga of transfers and postings begin.

It happens at less frequency and with less brazenness for the officers serving under the central government than those in the state governments.

At times, there appears to be a pre-decided thought process that civil servants or officers were not serving the people but their masters hence, they need to be transferred.

Sometimes such transfers and postings begin before the elections. The reasons are known to every common man. Often an honest and efficient government employee is harassed using this tool of frequent change in portfolios or transfers/postings.

I do not need to name some of the bureaucrats who have seen umpteen number of transfers at the behest of politicians – mind you, all in public interest – to less important portfolios. The aim behind such transfers may be to silence the voice that can create problems in 'managing governance'.

Some states and particularly departments under them are notorious for this game of transfers and postings.

Some of these departments include the Police (from senior officers to the lowest rank of *havaldar*), Hospitals (mainly doctors and professors engaged in teaching, but not limited to them), Commercial Tax or Value Added Tax, Excise, Regional Transport Office (RTO) and what not. The list is long.

There have been accusations against the government of a national party in the central state of Madhya Pradesh that engaged in large-scale transfers and postings. There were reports suggesting that those who offered were brought back and others who could not or did not, were made to move to the new place, far away from their existing place of posting.

Those who were at the fag end of their service were also not spared. No, when it comes to transfers, the system doesn't see gender – women employees were equal victims as men.

The state of affairs in Bihar, which arguably has been giving a large number of civil servants, is another unique case. There is so much to talk about Bihar, for its hard-working people who can be found employed in almost all parts of the country and in the world, and in almost all spheres of activity. Suffice it to cite the example of alleged irregularities in its health department. Bihar which faces shortage of doctors and teaching staff in medical colleges, like most other states, does not shy away from transfers and postings giving the convenient reasons of administrative exigencies or in 'public interest'.

Due unconditional apology to Madhya Pradesh and Bihar administration in case I have stepped on someone's feet. There are many departments and many tales to tell. But I have to limit my answer.

These transfers and postings, like many of the wrong doings in the Indian governance system, is an open secret and known to all, be it political party leaders, bureaucrats or the citizens at large.

I do not have a prejudiced approach towards this normal procedure of transfers and postings but would just like to point out the systemic faults.

In fact, having covered for long, anti-corruption related measures in governance, I am aware that the Government of India has a rotational transfer policy.

Besides, there exist directives from the CVC – the country's probity watchdog – yes "probity" watchdog, that mandates timely transfer of those working at sensitive posts to stem the possibility of corruption or any irregularities.

Transfers and postings to new places also help employees to gain diverse experience that helps the government and eventually governance. Similar directives exist for the state government employees by respective agencies.

Some of the state governments have also formed a civil services board to ensure that civil servants adhere to the minimum tenure policy or complete the minimum tenure stipulated for a particular post being held by them.

There is no dearth of rules and regulations to check these unlawful transfers and postings, but the political and administrative 'will' to stand for what is right is missing.

I strongly advocate 'fair implementation' of the rotational transfer-and-posting policy for bureaucrats and government employees. Political leaders like the chief ministers and the ministers concerned must keep a close watch that neither they nor any of their party leaders are able to wield their power to get into this nefarious game of transfers.

There are so many people who silently suffer due to frequent transfers. Their morale gets affected and they become less devoted and sincere towards the goal of public service.

Hope the governments, bureaucrats and politicians, take a balanced, judicious view and put a check on harassment of government employees through the magical wand of transfers and postings claiming they were done in 'public interest'.

Wish to see the houses in order!

Why is there a fascination among Indian youth towards becoming civil servants?

To be part of the country's civil services that has a rich tradition is really a matter of pride for one and all.

Being part of the coveted civil services has all that one desires for – name, fame, power of authority, job security and perks (both while in service and post-retirement).

All these exercise a significant influence in the minds of the youth while zeroing on a career. That is the reason we find lakhs of people taking the civil services exam year after year.

Most even leave high-paid jobs in the private sector to join the civil services.

A desire to bring positive change in the society and in the lives of common masses is another strong reason for many to join these prestigious public service jobs.

The intention of working for the people, however, is not experienced as one gets old in the system. That is the deleterious element of what the system does to civil servants.

The civil services in the country have not been undergoing many churns and changes and it is not going to lose its value any time soon.

Civil services are a powerful tool to work for the betterment of the society and the country.

However, such tools need to be used for the welfare of the people at large and not for serving vested interests for personal aggrandisement.

Having said that, it can be safely presumed that the fascination among youth to join civil services will only increase and the government should try to make it more rewarding to minimize instances of corruption and brain drain.

A serious attempt must be made to draw the best brains in the country as they form the bulwark of the administrative machinery. This is necessary to bring about positive changes in the lives of the common men and women of this country.

There is also a need to reform the recruitment process of the country's civil servants and its workforce. All suggestions and requests to bring about changes from aspirants and academicians are already in the public domain.

People concerned are aware of it. Many aspirants demand level-playing field while taking examinations for job recruitment. It is unfair to even consider that an engineer or somebody with a management degree or an English-speaking individual can be a good civil servant.

A Parliamentary panel in its report submitted to the Parliament in March 2021 had said that the chairperson and members of the UPSC should be persons of impeccable integrity, rectitude, high caliber and impartial.

The committee feels that the methodology followed for their selection should be fair, transparent and objective and also uphold the principles of social justice, diversity and gender equality, the Department-Related Parliamentary Standing Committee on Personnel, Public Grievances, Law and Justice had said in its 106th report on Demands for Grants (2021-22) of the Ministry of Personnel, Public Grievances and Pensions.

The UPSC conducts civil services examinations to select officers of the Indian Administrative Service (IAS), Indian Foreign Service (IFS) and Indian Police Service (IPS), among many others.

The UPSC changes the pattern of civil services examination from time to time on the basis of recommendations made by various expert committees.

"However, no study has been commissioned to assess how such changes impacted the aspirants, nature of recruitment and administration at large. In light of the above, the committee emphatically reiterates its recommendation and hopes that the Ministry (of Personnel) will accomplish the task at the earliest," the report had said.

The Committee had also asked the Staff Selection Commission (SSC) to spare no efforts to ensure the integrity of its examination process at all costs.

The SSC which conducts the largest number of selection for government jobs, is mandated to make recruitment to Group 'B' (non-Gazette) and Group 'C' (non-technical) posts in various ministries/departments of the Government of India and their attached and subordinate offices.

Are honest bureaucrats afraid of doing the right job due to fear of persecution from investigating agencies?

As the maxim goes, the honest need not fear the law but the dishonest should! It is a pity that an honest person has feelings of apprehension or fears probe agencies such as the CBI, Income Tax department, Enforcement Directorate (ED), *Lokpal* and the CVC. Thanks to so many governments which have come and gone but failed to instill confidence among those working with honesty and dedication.

We all know what happened in the coal scam (that made news in 2012) and the 2G spectrum allocation scam (that got public attention after the Comptroller and Auditor General (CAG) mentioned it in one of its reports tabled in the Parliament in 2010). Some of the bureaucrats named in these scams were exonerated by the courts.

There are more such cases, not as big as these, where bureaucrats had to fight a long battle after being framed by the prosecuting agencies.

There have also been cases where some of the officers, pretty senior ones, of the level of Secretary to the Government of India, who did not take any new innovative decision, rather took a safe decision, fearing harassment from these probe agencies. One of the officers concerned even joined the country's anti-corruption watchdog adding to the efficiency of the toothless tiger mandated to check corruption.

In the process, the country and the people inevitably suffered.

However, call it fear or lack of strong will, the perception of harassment from these probe-cum-prosecuting agencies exists in the hearts and minds of some honest bureaucrats. On the contrary, a not-so-honest one continues to line his pockets and goes scot free.

The fear of harassment from the central government's investigations is also never ruled out by businessmen.

The governments must take steps to instill confidence in the minds of most government employees and members of the business community that they won't be harassed.

The government has been sensitizing the civil servants/ government employees that their bona fide mistakes will be ignored and they will be protected. But perhaps more needs to be done as there is a yawning gap between precept and practice.

At the same time, there must be fear of the law (and also of anti-corruption agencies) in people so that they are deterred from doing anything immoral or illegal. The fear of law can be justly instilled through prompt and exemplary punishment to the guilty.

Would the corrupt let that happen is the challenge the government is struggling to find an answer to?

Why is there less representation of women in government jobs?

Seven decades after independence, the Indian society is not only still male dominated but all of them also consider themselves the alpha male.

Having more women in government offices could perhaps lead to less or no corruption as women are generally considered more scrupulous in their work and less corrupt than men.

Without going much into some of the practices that resulted in uneven gender balance and bias towards girls/women, it would suffice to say that there are socio-economic (more of social and less of economic) reasons to account for this imbalance.

The census of central government employees brought out by the Directorate General of Employment & Training, Ministry of Labour and Employment (MOLE), in 2011 had indicated the total number of employees in various central ministries/department as 30,87,278 out of which only 3,37,439 employees constituted women.

This was the information laid in Parliament by the Government of India in March 2020. The figure of women employment is self-explanatory. It was merely 10.92 per cent.

The situation has not changed much between 2011 and 2020. This is despite the fact that by and large girls have been outshining boys in schools, colleges and other competitive examinations by securing top ranks and acing all exams.

Women have consecutively topped the civil services

examinations in 2015, 2016 and 2017.

The government has been taking steps to provide all support that women may need while in service as a way to encourage them to join the workforce.

A typical line that is mentioned in the civil services examination notification every year is 'Government strives to have a workforce which reflects gender balance and that women candidates are encouraged to apply'.

However, the results are not satisfactory.

The hallmark of an egalitarian society would also be to ensure adequate representation of women in the country's workforce.

The government needs to come out with a new policy that encourages women to be part of its workforce.

The same should be extended to the private sector which witnesses a bias against employment of women. A strict check is required to rectify this imbalance and to give women their rightful place in the society.

Why women in sufficient numbers are not part of the government and private workforce despite being equally skilled as their counterparts is something the society and the governments need to ponder over and find a solution.

I, however, do not go with the perception of women being less corrupt than men. Corruption is an individual vice that doesn't discriminate with gender. Anyone can be corrupt and gender has nothing to do with it.

To sum up, governments and society must encourage women to take up employment and get equal opportunities at the workplace.

Employment conditions should not be too bureaucratic in the country, which is another cause of concern for many.

A society and ultimately the country will progress faster by the contribution of women as part of the workforce.

Noting that the percentage of women candidates to top managerial posts in public sector undertakings (PSUs) is abysmally low, a parliamentary committee has asked the government head hunter PESB to carry out an in-depth study. They will examine if this gender gap is due to scarcity of competent women aspirants or the glass ceiling effect, the Department-Related Parliamentary Standing Committee on Personnel, Public Grievances, Law and Justice said in its 106th report on Demands for Grants (2021-22) of the Ministry of Personnel, Public Grievances and Pensions.

The Committee is of the opinion that there is a need to build an equitable work place for women and PESB must make an endeavour in this regard, said the report tabled in Parliament in March 2021.

The Public Enterprises Selection Board (PESB) has been set up with the objective of evolving a sound managerial policy for the Central Public Sector Enterprises and in particular, advises the government on appointments to their top management posts.

Why do some government departments remain notorious for corruption despite harsh anti-corruption laws?

It is an open secret that some government departments and organizations are dens of corruption. These departments mock the government's claim of good governance free from corruption.

Go to majority of the regional transport offices (RTOs) to get a driving licence and you shall have a personalized experience of systemic corruption.

From touts standing outside the offices claiming quick

work on payment of hush money to a government employee sitting inside the office finding fault with your documentation in an obvious bid to help the touts, are some experiences.

At times, employees responsible for doing a job, in this case helping a man getting a licence, are not easily found at their desks. However, skilled and connected touts can locate their 'signal' and get them to the seat and ensure the work is done in the quickest possible time.

In India, one of the reasons (except alcohol) behind road accidents, poor driving skills and frequent jams on most of our roads is that majority of such licences are a 'gift' to the drivers – thanks to some corrupt RTOs and touts working there.

I don't have to narrate any instance to prove the truth of my assertion. All those who have been to a transport authority (majority of them, if not all) would vouch for this and give details of systemic corruption that exists even today.

A few RTOs may be exceptions, where much of the work is 'really digitized' and their systems do not get conked out too often. But I have my doubts over the efficiency!

Another hotbed of corruption is the 'registry office' – it is a revenue office dealing with registration of properties. One can witness structured corruption there. The efficiency of the staff in such offices is praise worthy , thanks to the motivation that they get other than the salary by the government.

Municipal corporations or associated offices in most Indian towns/cities tell the same frustrating and irritating tale of corruption.

All this goes under the very nose of the government that boasts of a zero tolerance policy towards corruption and claims that it can sniff out any corrupt activities and stem it.

Visit any office dealing with land records and town planning, responsible for approving building plans, in any district/state and one would be introduced to systemic corruption that takes place there.

An individual is made to grease the palm of the concerned people (at times entire chain from peon to approving officer) at these places to get their work done. A few state governments have introduced an online system for getting maps approved for the construction of buildings, but the 'indigenous human intelligence' has defeated this very online system to pave their way to get what they want.

Construction of road and tendering for different government works are two other areas badly affected by corruption. Who doesn't know the grave corruption in these works?

Why has corruption at such places not been stopped? Officers have come and gone but these departments have continued to follow the systematic corrupt practices for majority of the work. Nothing moves without money in such offices.

Solutions are many but takers/doers are a few.

I still wait in everlasting hope of a crusader, an officer, who on getting posted to any department tries to get rid of corruption (I sincerely hope that my pessimism is short-lived though!).

My worry is that such an officer would be moved to a less-important job in 'public interest' for displaying such courageous traits.

Why is the country's bureaucracy tainted with inefficiency, corruption and red-tape?

It is painful to know about the perception of bureaucracy that exists in the minds of the people.

What is even more painful is that this perception has travelled abroad and is carried by most people related to India.

As an Indian, it pains me the most. There is no denying the fact that governance, especially at the grass root level or for the not-so-well-off is still inaccessible.

Few exceptions could be the services which are digitally available like getting an Aadhaar or Permanent Account Number (PAN), among others.

This is because a computer programme doesn't discriminate. Most people are disappointed after visiting the government offices of the country.

The problem of the system lies with the system. There have been fewer efforts (if not none) in encouraging the staff (especially at the lower level who interact with the public or act as interface between the government and the people in general) for their work.

Such staff does not have the confidence that their sincere efforts in ensuring hassle-free public service delivery would be appreciated.

Often it has been noticed that a performer has been punished with more work rather than appreciated/out-of-turn promoted for the good work. The lack of encouragement and motivation is the foremost reason behind inefficiency and corruption in the government departments.

I would not elaborate on work shirkers and corrupt public servants. They are everywhere and need to be identified and removed.

It is also not the case that only the lower level staff (clerical or otherwise) at crucial levels of public dealing is corrupt or inefficient. Their seniors patronise such instances as either being part of the problem or by being mute spectators.

Nothing stops a senior government officer, managing a section, wing or department, to ensure that subordinates under him or her work properly and do not resort to corruption or cause inconvenience to the people.

Nothing except a lack of strong will and the absence of commitment towards the cause!

A tinge of the problem of corruption lies with the society as well. Public servants are not extraordinary human beings. They are from amongst us. The society, meaning we the people, needs to be ethical.

Honesty is an individual quality and a personal choice. It cannot be borrowed easily from the outside world. A public servant has to instill, protect and nurture it irrespective of the allurement and circumstances.

It is a must to ensure that the coming generation experiences an effective administration which is free from all ills.

Corruption and inefficiency can be checked if those having the responsibility to check it act on their responsibilities. Fear of law and prompt punishment can be quick deterrents.

How do we select sincere, dedicated, honest and innovative civil servants?

In India, bureaucrats, police officers and diplomats among others are chosen following a three-tier civil services examination. So it can be safely assumed that the best are shortlisted and selected for the job.

They are then trained at the prestigious training academy manned by the best minds – experienced bureaucrats. The procedure to train bureaucrats is well-defined and they are taught the best skills for running the administrative system.

Examination pattern and the training pedagogies are revised from time to time to meet the changing requirements of the bureaucratic system. Bureaucrats from some other countries also come to India for specialized training.

There is no dearth of experts and specialists in the best administrative practices to be drawn into the pool of the faculty.

Not many can genuinely find fault with our civil services exam pattern and the training methodology.

In addition, the government has been invoking rules that allow it to retire a 'deadwood' in public interest when such a person is found inefficient or corrupt.

The civil services examination has helped in giving so many bureaucrats who were/are meritorious, agile, innovative and efficient. Of course, this is possible only when they are not corrupt.

But the question still remains: How do we choose a bureaucrat who is incorruptible?

As has been mentioned earlier, corruptibility is a gene found in the DNA of most human beings. It gets activated and starts reacting when it finds a suitable host – an opportunity to exploit a system.

There exists no technique to help us look into a human being and prepare him as a good bureaucrat free from corruption and inefficiency.

India can perhaps, take a cue from Singapore and other nations as to how they have been able to manage an efficient bureaucracy. Singapore's model of efficient administration in the whole of South Asia and South-East Asia is a subject of another book.

However, to answer the question – how can the government keep the civil servants motivated – from the day they step into the training academy till they retire after completing their tenure.

They can be motivated by way of acknowledging their honest work (Prime Minister's award given annually to some bureaucrats for their outstanding work is a step in this direction), rewarding their honesty and stiffly punishing the corrupt so that efficient bureaucracy is encouraged.

One also has to check nepotism and favouritism in bureaucracy as that is one of the biggest stumbling blocks to a highly motivated and efficient workforce.

Good bureaucrats can flourish in the system provided they are given due recognition by those in authority and motivation for being efficient and creative. More importantly if they are kept away from unnecessary political interference.

Only then would they strive to work with dedication, as otherwise, they would also be part of the same coterie of bureaucrats whose presence has not helped the country much, except negatively, by spoiling the country's image in the eyes of the world.

All government employees need to be continuously encouraged to perform. They also need to be under check to ensure that they don't fall into the trap of any allurement or corruption.

The government should consider use of Artificial Intelligence in selecting, training and posting of government employees in India.

Government versus Private Sector

MOST people would agree that our governance 'model' is the best and that honest attempts have been made to continuously improve it to make it more people friendly.

I do not want to discredit these efforts from all stakeholders – politicians, public servants, civil society and journalists, among others.

However, there is a large scope for improvement and it is my firm belief the country/bureaucracy has all the means to achieve that feat.

Why are we still not able to attain that level of efficient governance that can make us all proud? The level where people don't have to stand in queues for long hours or face harassment in terms of rude behaviour, corruption or red-tape from the government employees for getting their work done.

The level where people have the confidence that their work will be done swiftly, without bribe? The level where people are treated equally by a government servant irrespective of his or her social/economic status?

The level, where industrialists have the confidence that they can get all government approvals, provided they have all the documents, without being victims of red-tape/corruption and without facing undue harassment?

I would like to reiterate that corruption, as I have already hinted in one of the earlier chapters, is not exclusive to the Indian administrative system, i.e. government departments/organizations.

Though, we being the 'developed' country and one of the most populous nations with 1.3 billion people (130 crore), are somehow badly affected due to our consistent failure in checking this persistent problem of corruption, which is more severe than COVID.

For a moment, let's also believe in the claims of those responsible for training bureaucrats or supervising them and agree that the country has best-in-class public servants, trained in all professional traits in the best of our institutions, filled with enthusiasm to bring change in the society, efficient, highly educated and non-corrupt.

Then why does development elude large swathes of our country? Why do we still hear cases of large-scale corruption, inefficiency, bureaucratic apathy and what not?

Most importantly, why don't we get the feel of a big multinational company (MNC) like governance that we often talk about and yearn for?

For instance, compare the functioning of state owned banks with the private ones. A lot of difference can be seen in the efficiency, workplace atmosphere and service delivery of employees working with private banks and those in government owned lending institutions.

It is not about dearth of talent, money for boosting infrastructure and reach of government banks or ideas. Bank employees in state owned institutions are selected through a tough examination procedure. They are equally talented if not superior to their counterparts in the private sector.

The intention behind mentioning this example is not to look down upon them or to criticize them, but to draw a comparison.

Same is the case with those in our postal department, especially those involved in public dealing. Compare their working with those in the leading courier/cargo companies of the private sector.

The difference is already known to most of us.

See the size and extent and reach of our postal department. Infrastructure-wise, money-wise and manpower-wise, we are second to none. Our postmen deliver letters and money to people living even in the remotest corners of the country, at high altitudes and valleys.

Their services are cost-effective too compared to their private counterparts. Despite this salient difference, the 'service' satisfaction of the state owned postal department doesn't meet people's expectations or the desired standards.

During the pursuit of my professional work, I have come across a number of bureaucrats – highly talented, multi-taskers, energetic, raring to bring about a change in the society. However, their eagerness takes a back seat in this too-Indianised bureaucratic system, which is still miles and seas away from meeting people's expectations of bridging the governance gap that hurts our country.

So the question arises, how can we get rid of the malaise

that ails the system? Why do civil servants individually and collectively fail to deliver the real good governance that we all aspire for?

What is it that ails the country's bureaucracy and results in negative perception in the minds of the people at large?

Why are people not happy and are wary of visiting a government office for their work?

Why is governance still inaccessible to many?

These are some of the common problems besides the decades old problem of corruption and red tapism.

The assertion-cum-analysis is in the following chapter. It is based on 'self experience' and on the basis of threadbare discussion/analysis I had with subject experts, academicians, former and serving bureaucrats, journalists and social activists all of whom for understandable reasons, have chosen to remain anonymous.

What Ails Bureaucracy?

THE Indian governance system has most of the provisions that one can think of to deliver good governance. What's tragic is that they are mostly on papers and rarely translate into reality.

There is a lack of will and commitment from many stakeholders in walking the extra mile for the betterment of the people and eventually the country.

Increased use of technology and Artificial Intelligence in public service delivery is the need of the hour.

Bureaucracy is in dire need of radical changes through timely, frequent and continuous 'surgical strikes' to meet the aspirations of the people of new India that the present government also envisages to achieve.

The ailments of bureaucracy are contagious, more communicable than the novel coronavirus and it is fast affecting the people of the country.

Needless to say the perception of bureaucracy among most parts of our country is not satisfactory. It is also affecting the country's image outside India.

I do feel immensely sad while mentioning this perception

(which is the reality in most parts of the country), as I know some officers/government employees who toil day in and day out in the service of the nation and its people.

They do make sincere efforts, to the best of their ability given the limitations, and have been able to achieve considerable success.

Going back to the main topic of the bureaucracy's ailments, I have been able to discuss some of the causes behind it with subject experts including serving and retired civil servants, social activists and academicians.

These ailments are classified and explained as follows:

Lacks innovation

Most of the government employees woefully lack motivation, passion and hunger for innovation. Many of them, when they join the service, have their motivational level at a peak.

However, one notices that their passion and urge to innovate invariably tends to wither with the passage of time.

What is worrying is that they stop improving upon honing their skills and upgrading their knowledge.

Why does motivation and passion evaporate with time? Could it be due to complacency, monotony, callousness or feeling of security which a government job gives them? Why cannot learning and skill-upgrade become an essential part of all categories of government employees and not limiting to officers only?

In most organizations, there are visible signs of lack of motivation in the employees eager to work. Employees are not encouraged to innovate or work passionately.

At times, an out-of-the-box working pedagogy is

discouraged by seniors merely for the reason that it is unusual.

Governance is people friendly when innovative ways are invented and implemented passionately by a motivated workforce.

New working methods and ways to work efficiently need to be discovered, promoted and encouraged for the larger good of the people.

Those showing passion to work efficiently, diligently and meticulously are sidelined. The reason behind this is an open secret for all.

Why don't we ever hear a story of innovation by an employee working at the level of a peon, support staff or at a clerical post?

Why does the country's administrative system neglect grass-root innovations and innovative thinking by these categories of employees?

Should continuous upgrading of skills and a 'real and effective assessment' of the employees' performance be made a pre-requisite for promotions/career growth especially at the lower cadre like those working as peons, support staff, clerks and other such key positions?

Lacks professionalism

This may be considered an unusual concern for the country's elite and mammoth bureaucracy that already faces many challenges, most of which are self-inflicted.

Lack of professionalism exists in a real and palpable way and affects not only civil servants but the entire class of government employees, working with either the centre or state governments.

Professionalism can be explained as competence or skill that one possesses while doing his work. It is the conduct that one manifests while working.

An employee, irrespective of his or her level, is expected to show professionalism in all stages of work life. However, this is not seen widely in the Indian *babudom.*

Discount it as a pity problem or not that important aspect, but in reality employees (hence the organization's) efficiency is affected and gauged by the way they behave with the citizens, especially the downtrodden ones, who approach them for work.

The perception most people carry about the country's governance/government organizations is mainly due to the lack of professionalism among employees.

The comparison between private and government sector is often cited due to this impolite behaviour. People praise and prefer the private sector not because their services are cheap or best, but they find hassle free access to it contrary to the government departments where one has to face tantrums and procrastination from those at the seat.

Most of the government employees instead of being courteous to the common people, who approach them for government work, act in a non-cordial and non-professional way.

There is also absence of an effective system in these organizations to report such unprofessional behavior. One would only report such behavior to the delinquent employee's superior when he is assured of just action and hassle free access to such authority.

Red Tapism

This is omnipresent in the context of the Indian bureaucratic system. Red-tape or the collective term – red tapism, is the biggest culprit behind all problems and ailments associated with good governance.

The mysterious maze of the Indian file system is a matter of great research. How a file keeps rotating in a 'bureaucratic orbit' (as mentioned in one of the earlier chapters) due to red-tapism is beyond anyone's comprehension.

It breaks the pace of service delivery and the country's efforts towards achieving the goal of good governance. How even a simple work can be delayed and left undone for years due to some English-era rule is evident to the people who visit most of the country's government offices.

Why cannot work process be made faster in all the government departments, especially those related to public service delivery?

Why is file movement not completely digitized yet?

Why are most public service delivery matters processed manually?

Many people in the country are frustrated victims of red-tapism that delays their work, almost daily.

Lack of digitization

There is an urgent need to ensure 100 per cent digitization of government work, especially related to public service delivery. Some state governments have taken steps in this direction. But since the system is not completely automated yet, it is misused by some to abuse gullible people.

It is beyond my comprehension to understand the delay in ensuring digitization of most of the work that may warrant people's interaction with the *babus* or require visiting government offices.

In this digital era, people must have a choice to do all their work online if they are well-versed with the technology and capable of affording it. Physical visit to an office or a facilitation centre should continue to be an option.

The government must put in place a robust information technology based infrastructure to support such modern-age mechanism of public service delivery. It will help in checking corruption and keep at bay the red-tape.

In addition, there should also be a fear of prompt punishment in the hearts and minds of wrong doers.

Many in civil services or in governance say they fear the three Cs – usually referred to the Central Bureau of Investigation or CBI, which is the country's federal probe agency, the country's anti-corruption watchdog the Central Vigilance Commission (CVC), and the Comptroller and Auditor General or CAG of India mandated with audit of government departments.

On the contrary, I feel such fear at times leads to efficiency and also keeps a check on corrupt employees.

Priority to output and not outcome

There could be at least two easy ways to gauge one's efficiency – by output or by outcome.

Most of the country's workforce in government establishments is concerned about the output which could be certain bureaucratic parameters.

They are least worried about the outcome which is the real matrix to assess a government employee or an organization's success.

Civil servants need to be outcome-oriented instead of delivering some output. Whether or not one does any constructive work would definitely be some output, but it may not yield the right outcome.

This approach is affecting the working of government employees and ultimately the people who fail to enjoy the benefits of good governance.

Also, most of the employees, especially those at the senior level, go strictly by the rule book.

There is a need to make some modifications and bring in innovations as there cannot be one-size-fits-all kind of solution for governance related issues in a vast country like ours.

Peter Principle

The Peter Principle was coined by psychologist Laurence J Peter and Raymond Hull in 1969. In common parlance, the principle is phrased as 'employees tend to rise to their level of incompetence'.

Employees should not only be promoted because they are working in a particular organization or in a role for long.

Promotion must be on the basis of performance. No performance, no promotion should be the new mantra for the government. The performance of employees needs to be assessed fairly and in a just manner.

Sincere efforts need to be made to guard departments and employees against the operation of the Peter Principle. This is an important reason that cripples the delivery of good governance and de-motivates performing employees.

Lack of good pay, perks and a well-defined career progression acts as key reasons for lack of motivation among the workforce of the government sector.

Those putting in sincere, honest and dedicated efforts are not rewarded appropriately in government organizations.

I feel all categories of government employees are not adequately paid in proportion to the work done by them. This I say for honest and hard working employees, who do exist in the government but are not in abundance. The division of work needs to be carefully charted. Few should not be burdened with all the work for being performers.

Career progression is not well-defined and followed in letter and spirit. Most of the performing workforce is devoid of their rightful due, most probably for being sincere.

I am aware of the government's budgetary constraints and pay-panel recommendations that invariably claim to recommend best-in-the-industry (or world) salary and allowances for the country's bureaucrats/employees.

There also has to be pay parity between those in government jobs with those engaged in the private sector.

Air-conditioned governance

Many government employees, especially those at the level of officers, suffer from this 'air-conditioned working syndrome'.

Despite the benefits of field visit that they are made aware of during their training days and initial postings, most of the civil servants are not aware of ground realities that are in need of drastic changes.

Field visits and direct feedback from the ground by those in power helps in improving governance.

There would be gaps if decision making is done based on the feedback received from experts or 'trusted officers', who most of the time are ignorant of the ground realities.

Senior employees must ensure they do field visits periodically, if not frequently, and the findings which could help in improving governance may be put in the public domain along with the action taken.

They should also ensure that the staff under them goes for regular field visits to the concerned areas to understand the problems and challenges at the ground level and to find solutions for the same.

Imagine the drastic change in the lives of the people when the government will be reaching out to them for their work, through electronic medium of communication or through in-person visits.

Trust deficit

There exists trust deficit between officers from central civil services and those from state civil services. My experience has been that officers from state civil services are equally talented and skilled as those in central civil services. However, the general perception is that officers from All India Services – Indian Administrative Service (IAS), Indian Police Service (IPS) and Indian Forest Service (IFoS) – tend to overlook talent in state civil services, when they are posted in a particular state. This inadvertent behavior discourages skilled officers from state civil services.

Those from state civil services are in no way less efficient or allegedly corrupt. They are talented with a strong knowledge of governance related ailments that affect the people of the state they live or work in. At times I feel these officers can really come up with solutions to most of the governance related problems faced by people as they are connected to ground realities.

This trust deficit among officers of the central and state civil services results in lack of coordination and efficiency thus, defeating the very purpose of good governance. Let there be camaraderie and coordination between the officers of central and state civil services.

Most civil servants consider junior staff as less capable. This feeling demotivates the junior staff. Conscious efforts need to be put in by the government officers to ensure that the employees under them continue to perform and shine in their careers.

Government officers must hand-hold junior staff and act as mentors to push them to deliver.

How about ranking of efficient government wings on the basis of outcome and not on output?

Another test case could be to bring employees from state governments on short-term 'in-office' training to central government and vice versa. Rules and norms at present may not allow this but it has potential to be a game changer and may bring expected reforms in the bureaucracy. Some employees from the state governments still vie for working in Delhi, the seat of power.

Centralization of Power

India has a three-tier governance structure: Centre, State and *Panchayati Raj*. There is need to ensure functional autonomy at each of these three levels. At present, there are sufficient instances to show that decision making is not decentralized.

Take the example of a DM or District Magistrate (also known as Collector). It is a crucial post for a person/officer in the Indian governance system. He is considered the king of a district, literally! Nothing moves, administrative-wise, without the approval of a DM.

There appears to be over reliance on a DM for each and

every work, probably owing to traces continuing in the country's governance system since the colonial era. The primary job of a Collector is to look after revenue collection, which is the main task for ensuring economic development.

There are other important policy making tasks assigned to a DM. He acts as an executive magistrate and is responsible for almost all things of a district, a large area under him.

There exists growing discontent among officers/employees of different government departments, like those incharge of running the district hospital or looking after district education, over the alleged interfering role played by a DM.

There is a need to ensure decentralization of power and to confirm that all organs of a district work independently. The supervision and coordination may be done by a DM or Collector but it must be ensured that such exercise is not construed as transgression.

(Over dependence on the IAS is explained in a separate chapter in the book)

Similarly, efforts need to be made to decentralize decision making at appropriate levels. It will make decision making and implementation faster. If done properly, such decentralization of administrative and financial power can check systemic corruption as well.

Corruption

Besides these broad causes behind the poor image of bureaucracy/administration, there is an age-old ailment of petty and large scale corruption.

Writing about it would perhaps be stating the obvious and questioning the herd immunity which has been developed by the 'doers' (those in position) and the 'bearers' (common men, victims of such vices)!

I have already described need-based and greed-based corruption in the Indian administrative system in one of the previous chapters.

Suffice to say that consistent efforts need to be made to ensure that officers/employees don't abuse their position to mint money or extort monetary benefits from common people who may contact them for getting their work done.

The country would be immensely benefitted if corruption is checked to 50 per cent of what exists as of now!

Data 'mis-entry'

BOTH the central and state governments run different schemes for people's welfare. People also need to get certain official IDs/ documents to get access to a host of government services.

For instance, Aadhaar (the 12-digit unique number issued by the Unique Identification Authority of India or the UIDAI) has been made (*almost) mandatory for people for a large number of schemes/facilities.

Aadhaar is needed for getting a bank account opened and for passport application, among other services.

Similarly, a Permanent Account Number (PAN) issued by the Income Tax department is required for opening a Demat account (short for dematerialization account for holding stock market securities), filing of returns, purchase of property and for doing other financial transactions.

An Elector Photo Identity Card (EPIC) is issued by the Election Commission of India for eligible voters.

* I say so as Aadhaar is compulsory in practice but may not be so in black and white.

An identity card is also issued for eligible beneficiaries of the Central Government Health Scheme (CGHS).

Such identity cards or documents issued by the government entities are needed by most of the individuals for work, investment, identification, address proof or foreign travel.

These documents are also required for getting benefits under the welfare schemes implemented by the government.

All these are important documents and help people in ease of living. However, there are instances of data entry errors in processing these identity cards. It may sound a small or insignificant concern but has wide ramifications.

I have seen so many people applying online for correction or queuing up outside government offices to fix such data errors or 'mis' entries.

What is frustrating is that in a majority of cases they were victims of data 'mis'entry by those feeding the data. It becomes highly inconvenient for people to revisit the formalities in order to fix the incorrect data in their identity cards.

At times, somebody's name or address gets misspelt on Aadhaar or EPIC. From incorrect mentioning of date of birth, age, gender to family details (spouse, mother and father as the case may be) an individual faces any or all of these mostly due to error in data entry.

(I myself have been a victim of data 'mis'entry and can very well imagine the pain and agony one undergoes to get the corrections done).

In most cases, all these errors happen at the entry level, that is by the person feeding the data.

The carelessness in data entry is a national problem and it has spread its tentacles to the private sector as well (wrong entry in health or insurance policy among others).

I would not say that it is done on purpose but it is a major reason affecting good governance initiatives. It can also be held responsible for creating a negative perception about the country's governance system as almost everyone needs such documents with correct entries related to their personal details.

Why is it difficult to mention the name, address, family and required personal details correctly in the government database or on identity cards/official documents issued by the authorities?

Is it lack of alertness (if not carelessness), overburdened and unskilled data entry operators or demotivation that results in wrong entries that create problems for the common man. This opens up avenues for touts/corrupt officers to cash in from those who do not have access to the right people or resources to raise grievances against it?

Most of the governance related problems that is creating this negative image of the country's governance system, can be rectified if those incharge of feeding in the data for issuing government documents (be it Aadhaar or EPIC or any other) are more careful.

Senior officials and supervisors need to pay urgent and special attention to this aspect to ensure good governance.

A considerable number of people in this country may not have uniformity of name and other details in their identity cards/relevant government documents mainly due to avoidable data entry errors.

People also need to be cautious while filling up application forms either online or offline.

One of the ways is to have a fully digitized system that

pops up a replica of the identity cards/government documents that are being issued by the concerned authority at the time of application itself.

This measure is being followed by the Ministry of External Affairs (MEA) while accepting applications for issuance of passport online.

One gets to know what major details his or her passport would have post its issuance. It does away with the possibility of data errors that might happen in manual feeding of the data.

UIDAI, Income Tax department and the Election Commission of India may also consider such facilities for issuance of Aadhaar, PAN and EPIC, respectively. Such and other changes would change the face of governance.

There is a need for the government organizations to learn from each other and improve. Good governance practices being followed by a department need to be followed by others doing similar work.

One of the examples is UIDAI and the Election Commission of India. An individual can get a duplicate Aadhaar card by payment of a fee online at his or her registered address in the UIDAI's records.

However, at present there is no such facility (as of March 2021) that allows an individual to get his or her EPIC or voter ID card on payment of fees online.

Why such a facility has not been started by the Election Commission is really a matter of concern?

Digitization, with zero human interference, would be a game changer for the country. People suffer and blame government authorities for corruption, red tapism and error in data entry as most of the public services are partially digitized with human (government employee/officer) intervention.

The country needs to completely digitize all public service deliveries with no human interference else business as usual would sadly continue!

From issuance of identity cards and official documents to getting them corrected, putting all these works in an online frame would help the people immensely.

IAS - The Super Service?

IT is widely considered that the officers of the Indian Administrative Service (IAS) run this huge country.

The IAS is the most prestigious and sought-after civil service of the country. Most people taking the civil service examination aspire to join it.

According to the Personnel Ministry, the IAS was constituted in 1946. Prior to that, the Indian Imperial Service (1893-1946) was in force.

The functions of an IAS officer broadly include:

- Collection of revenue and function as courts in revenue matters
- Function as executive magistrate
- Supervision of implementation of policies of state and central governments
- Travel to places to oversee implementation of policies
- In the process of policy formulation and decision making, IAS officers at various levels like Joint Secretary, Deputy Secretary etc. make their contributions and give final shape to policy

- Handle daily affairs of the government, including framing and implementation of policy in consultation with the minister-in-charge of the concerned ministry*

It is fairly easy to gauge the kind of power that has been bestowed on an IAS officer to carry out different functions.

However, there are different tales of alleged monopoly or domination exercised by this elite group.

A Parliamentary panel has in its report tabled in Parliament in March 2021, said that the Indian administration has become heavily dependent upon a particular administrative service and it is time to give equal opportunity to officers belonging to other services having expertise in that specific domain.

The committee said it is of the view that while making appointments to higher echelons of the administration priority should be given to integrity, caliber, aptitude and interest of the officer among other things, rather than the service to which he belongs.

"The generalist versus specialist controversy is one of the major challenges facing the Indian civil service. Today, India needs no generalists or specialists but specialized generalists, i.e. a generalist with knowledge and work experience in a particular domain. This calls for administrative review and restructuring along functional lines," the report had said.

The committee is of the opinion that the Indian administration has become heavily dependent upon a particular

---

* The aforesaid function and other details have been sourced from an official document 'IAS Service Profile' of the Personnel Ministry.

administrative service, the Department-related Parliamentary Standing Committee on Personnel, Public Grievances, Law and Justice had said in its 106th report on Demands for Grants (2021-22) of the Ministry of Personnel, Public Grievances and Pensions.

"They seem to have an edge over others in securing key decision making positions in the government," it said, without mentioning the name of any service.

The panel's recommendation assumes significance as Prime Minister Narendra Modi said what can be achieved by handing over the nation to '*babus*' (government officials).

Just because somebody is an IAS officer, he is running fertiliser and chemical factories to airlines, Modi had said in a reference to public sector units being headed by bureaucrats, and asked what this will achieve.

The assertion by the Prime Minister on the IAS is for every one of us to analyze and decipher.

There are 5,166 IAS officers working across the country as against their sanctioned strength of 6,746, according to an official data.

The Seventh Central Pay Commission (CPC) in its report submitted to the government in November 2015 had mentioned that "other All India Services and various central services have all along been demanding parity with the IAS (and the IFS) and for removal of this conventional edge in pay and promotions".

As per the extant rules the Indian Administrative Service and the Indian Foreign Service (which are central Group `A' Services) are accorded a pay advantage, or an 'edge' at three grades, viz., the Senior Time Scale, Junior Administrative Grade and Selection Grade in the form of two additional increments at 3 per cent each, over and above the promotional increment.

Both services have traditionally enjoyed this edge vis-à-vis other All India and central services. This has continued right from the time of the first CPC with varying amounts.

Prior to the implementation of the Kothari Commission recommendations, the scheme of examination was so designed that an IAS or IFS aspirant had to appear for two additional papers with at least one paper from outside the field of his special study at the University, unless the candidate held a Master's or Honours degree in two subjects, the report said.

Thus, an IAS/IFS candidate had to appear in five papers as opposed to three papers in the case of central service aspirants or two by the Indian Police Service aspirants. However, the examination pattern, post 1979, became uniform for all services, it said.

The argument for continuance of edge has been that the role of IAS is still very important in the overall scheme of governance and that they have a multi-functional and integrating role in the administrative framework, the report had said.

Various central services have contended that this edge given to the IAS and the IFS is iniquitous and violates the principle of 'equal pay for equal work'.

They pointed out that the Civil Services Examination (CSE) conducted by the UPSC is common for recruitment to around 18 Group `A' Services and that the choice of service exercised by the candidates is based upon many factors.

It is not necessary that only the top-most go to the IAS. It has also been pointed out that officers of most of the services are, in their early years, posted to small places and subjected to many transfers. Therefore, the grant of an edge is seen as unfair, it had said highlighting the background.

The chairman of the panel had in the report said that the fundamental principle for determining the remuneration for any position is that it should be based on the complexity and difficulty of the duties and responsibility of the job in question.

The criticality of functions at the district administration level holds good equally for the IAS, IPS as well as the IFoS. Therefore, some additional remuneration, in the early stages of their career indeed is justified not only for the IAS but also for the IPS and IFoS, he said.

"Therefore, the edge presently accorded to the Indian Administrative Service at three grades mainly Senior Time Scale, Junior Administrative Grade and Selection Grade may continue in the form of two additional increments at 3 per cent each in the proposed pay matrix. The same is being recommended for the Indian Police Service and Indian Forest Service as well. In so far as the Indian Foreign Service is concerned, the existing dispensation shall continue," the report had said.

The reason behind mentioning the excerpts of the seventh Central Pay Commission's report is to highlight the importance and edge accorded to the Indian Administrative Service.

There has been discontentment among different services over this edge and other career benefits enjoyed by the IAS officers (and also by those in Indian Forest Service).

The problem aggravates as the officer steps up in service. There have been complaints of delay from the officers of other civil services (barring the IAS and the IFS) in empanelment for holding senior level posts in the Government of India.

There have been accusations from the officers of other civil services of delay in their empanelment, promotion and posting due to alleged systemic interference of the IAS officers at crucial decision making posts.

Almost all files related to senior level empanelments/promotions/postings have to go through a few gates, each of which is manned by IAS officers.

The IAS seems to be the intentional or unintentional preferred choice when it comes to managing a government office. Not only this, most of the secretary-level (top echelon of the *babu's* hierarchy) or head of department (HoD) posts are manned by officers of the IAS.

Why cannot officers from other services be made incharge of the concerned wing of the government despite holding necessary experience?

For example, why cannot officers of the Indian Information Service (IIS) be made secretary of the Ministry of Information and Broadcasting?

Why cannot an Indian Revenue Service officer be made secretary of the Department of Revenue?

Similarly, why cannot an officer of the Indian Audit and Accounts Service (IAAS) rise up to the level of Comptroller and Auditor General (CAG) of India?

There may be more such examples.

The moot point is, should dependence over IAS be balanced?

The 'System' and COVID-19

COVID-19 or the latest variant of the novel coronavirus caught most of the country unaware. An unknown virus, whose composition, cause and deadly effects were not known until it started taking toll on people beginning January 2020.

How did it start?

World Health Organization or WHO's country office in the People's Republic of China picked up a media statement by the Wuhan Municipal Health Commission from their website on cases of 'viral pneumonia' in Wuhan, according to the WHO's update of December 31, 2019, posted on its website.

Following which, the WHO requested information on the reported cluster of atypical pneumonia cases in Wuhan from the Chinese authorities, as per the update of January 1, 2020.

WHO tweeted that it had received the genetic sequences for the novel coronavirus from the People's Republic of China and expected these to soon be made publicly available, according to the update of January 11, 2020.

Chinese media reported the first death from the novel coronavirus, as per the WHO's update of January 11, 2020.

As the virus and its infection spread, India reported its first case of COVID-19 in late January 2020.

Since then different measures have been taken by both the central and state governments to contain its spread, including the nationwide lockdown announced in late March 2020 by Prime Minister Narendra Modi.

There has been a non-uniform pattern of effects and after-effects of COVID-19 cases and related deaths. Most parts of the country reported increase in the number of positive cases and deaths due to it since mid-March 2021.

India also started a nationwide vaccination programme starting with targeted groups, i.e. health care and frontline workers. Subsequently from May 1, 2021, the vaccination was opened to people of 18 years and above.

The Problem

There have been countless stories of trauma, mismanagement of resources, black marketing of drugs for use in the treatment of COVID patients, shortage of oxygen for patients under treatment at different private and government run hospitals that resulted in deaths of many, fires at hospitals treating COVID patients, busting of illegal factories selling fake injections by touting them as a cure to COVID and what not.

Some patients died as they could not get timely medical attention due to the shortage of beds/treatment facilities at various hospitals.

Some stories of pain and loss of loved ones brought tears to many eyes.

Crematoriums and burial grounds ran short of space. People were denied a dignified cremation in some cases, in different parts of the country.

In some reported cases, family members could not see the face of their deceased members as there were medical protocols for dealing with those who died due to COVID-19.

People also claimed difficulties in taking vaccination mainly due to non-availability of doses.

All eligible people are required to take two shots of the COVID vaccine after a gap of a certain number of days, depending on the type of vaccine administered.

There were tragic miseries in the air for most part of March and May 2021 in the country as though clouds and air were carrying the tears and pain of helpless and hapless people. Words cannot describe the situation that was witnessed in India during the pandemic.

It is hard to control when you have to talk about the pain and suffering of fellow human beings during the corona times.

If words could describe the situation during the worst phases of the pandemic they would be traumatic, painful and tearful.

What is the 'system'?

Coming back to the topic of the chapter, one common word that bore the brunt of people's grouse during the pandemic was the 'system'.

There was widespread criticism of the 'system' from one and all. 'System' is often referred to as the state of affairs or governance in a jurisdiction especially in the Indian context.

People blamed the governments, be it the centre or the

states, for their consistent failure in ensuring medical help, availability of medicines, oxygen and other drugs required for their treatment and for lockdown-like restrictions that resulted in price rise and unavailability of essential food items in most parts of the country due to hoarding and black marketing.

The 'system', according to many, is the government run by politicians and *'babus'* or bureaucrats.

Collectively, the employees and politicians like the PM and his council of ministers (in case of central/federal level) and Chief Minister and the ministers (in case of states/province level), among others, form the 'system' or the government.

Why was the 'system' blamed for people's miseries?

It is the government's duty to ensure that people's basic needs of food, clothes and shelter are taken care of.

Most people lost lives of their near and dear ones, struggled hard to get basic amenities in a just manner – getting RTPCR or Reverse Transcription Polymerase Chain Reaction test to check COVID, beds in hospitals and ventilator support for their kith and kin infected with the coronavirus.

People could not even find an ambulance for their loved ones who struggled with the virus, as they were not available due to the increased demand or their charges were exorbitant.

People also complained of hassles in ensuring dignified last rites of their loved ones who lost their battle to this deadly virus as most of the crematoriums or burial houses were running over their capacity.

Migrant labourers and daily wagers were badly hit as the lockdown restrictions resulted in closure of various industrial units, offices or other activities that brought employment.

As a result, they had to move out of cities to their native places, that too hurriedly. Lack of buses and trains, coupled with unexpectedly high fares, made the journey to their native place a herculean task.

How did most of these people look after their family after losing their jobs or having no place to work?

They all blamed these miseries on the 'system'. Rightfully so, as they were denied basic amenities and the threat of survival loomed large over them.

Could the 'system' have averted these miseries?

Ideally yes. Realistically, very difficult!

The government or the 'system' was caught off guard though they did their best to tide over the challenges thrown at them by the COVID-19 pandemic.

There was visible absence of a crisis management group (not that the country did not have one) that could have acted swiftly and brought some positive changes on the ground, many believed.

It appeared that certain organs of the government were working in silos rather than coordinating with each other to give a better response to the pandemic induced challenges.

The 'system' failed to apprehend beforehand that there would be movement of migrant labourers and loss of jobs.

That there would be disruption of economic activities thus, hurting the employment scenario in the country and rendering a large number of people without work and place to stay and with no food.

It failed to give confidence to people losing jobs or their near and dear ones to the virus, that their needs and concerns would be taken care of or that they would be addressed without delay.

What could have been done?

The government is supposed to be proactive and responsive.

One is always at an advantageous position when it comes to guiding the government. Such guidance is necessary to inform the decision makers about the alternatives that might have skipped their mind while battling with thousands of challenges.

I always believe that there are government employees (there are private employees too and I will also talk about them) who lack the sense of belonging to the country and its people. It is the sense of belonging that encourages them to walk the extra mile to do something worthwhile for the country and its people.

Government employees follow the written working code (do's and don'ts), rules and procedures. Should rules be modified for the ease of working? That would be a matter of discussion and debate.

Unprecedented public health emergency like the one noticed during the COVID-19 pandemic warrants innovative and prompt responses.

Take the example of deaths of patients in both government and private run hospitals. Why should people die of lack of oxygen when the country has the life saving gas in abundance?

Why should people face difficulty in getting life saving drugs and other medicines (like those for enhancing Vitamin C and Zinc), despite the fact that India is number one in manufacturing drugs?

Why should people face difficulty in getting their RTPCR or CT scan among other tests at the government hospitals when government claims of having sufficient funds to meet any eventuality?

Why should people die of hunger when the country's agriculture production is capable of feeding its population?

Why should people face difficulty in reaching their native place when India boasts of having wide rail and road networks?

Why should people be forced to pay inflated fare for their movement, especially during the COVID-19 induced lockdown?

Why couldn't a District Magistrate (DM) or a Collector, who is the administrative head of a district, stop forced migration of labourers?

Why couldn't the government make visible efforts to ensure that nobody in a district sleeps hungry or is devoid of basic medical attention?

There are many 'Whys?'

I would stop as the purpose of mentioning these miseries here is not to find fault with the 'system' but to tell those with power that how and where they failed in checking these miseries of the common man.

The government should have invoked its power and made sure that those fleecing people by selling medicines or providing beds in a hospital at skyrocket costs were treated harshly.

A DM or Collector should have stopped the migrant labourers from leaving the cities, apparently due to sheer panic and lack of food/shelter, and helped them with the necessary basic amenities.

The railways, a public sector behemoth, should have run sufficient free trains, of course with necessary COVID-related precautions, for labourers to select places to ensure that women and children do not face any trouble in reaching their native home towns.

Government organizations did not run sufficient number of special buses to ferry these workers to their native places.

Efforts should have been made in providing medicines and other medical equipment to those in need by appointing nodal officers to act between the company manufacturing them and a hospital (or a group of hospitals). Some states did appoint nodal officers. Could their appointment check the fleecing? This poser has already been answered by people in the country who had faced such problems.

Conclusion

Citing excuses and difficulty that might exist on ground or act as a hurdle may be considered easy. But the easiest is not to act when one is expected to do so.

The government machinery was ill-prepared for public health emergencies. They could not foresee or be ready for the worst effects of the pandemic. Even if they did foresee, as some may counter, they failed to devise a foolproof system to ensure that medical infrastructure should be able to sustain the kind of pressure it could face.

One may attribute it to shortage of resources or capabilities of the people concerned, but the truth is that those in power could not act in a way that would have reduced people's misery.

People made money out of this adversity by selling fake drugs, selling medicines at higher cost, charging inflated fee for hospital admission and nursing charges, conducting tests in an unprofessional manner and charging unfair high rates and by whatever means.

The mismanagement of response to COVID-19 pandemic related challenges is a collective failure. The government employees, being the custodians of decision making, were solely responsible for the delayed and much criticized responses to the problems faced by the people.

The buck also stops at 'we, the people,' some of who did not fulfill their constitutional mandate prescribed for the citizens of India.

I am sure a bitter lesson has been learnt by the nation in the form of miseries witnessed during the pandemic and the system and its organs (bureaucracy) gearing-up to respond to such challenges in an expected way.

To conclude, I would reiterate the government (that means all its organs, especially the decision makers) needs to be proactive, innovative and responsive to counter any public health emergency. We, the people, should also not be spared from failing to shoulder our responsibilities towards fellow countrymen, especially the less-privileged ones, in times of crises, like the COVID-19 pandemic.

Stories of Innovation and Courage

IT is not that exceptional work is not being done across the country by civil servants/government employees. But the same good work could not be carried forward by others in different parts of the country, which probably needed them badly.

There are many tales of innovation and good governance by civil servants and all other categories of government employees.

Some get rewarded but many remain limited to the area/state or domain as the case may be.

Many bureaucrats have been appreciated by the Prime Ministers (former and current) of the country for doing commendable work in improving the administration and promoting ease of governance by taking several good steps.

The central government honours civil servants every year with the Prime Minister's Awards for Excellence in Public Administration.

These awards are given during the Civil Services Day celebrations on April 21.

Background to the Awards Scheme

The Government of India instituted 'The Prime Minister's Awards for Excellence in Public Administration' in 2006 to acknowledge and reward the extraordinary and innovative work done by districts/organizations of the central and state governments.

This awards scheme was restructured in 2014 for recognizing the performance of District Collectors in the central government's priority programs and innovations in aspirational districts.

The scheme was restructured again in 2020, to recognize the performance of District Collectors towards economic development of the districts, among other parameters.

A number of civil servants have been honoured with these coveted awards for their matchless work worthy of emulation in other parts of the country.

However, it still remains a mystery as to why these award winning initiatives have not been adopted in other parts of the country.

Some of the work done by these civil servants had (still have) the potential to change the landscape of the country's socio-political development, if they were imbibed by their colleagues and worked upon, fine-tuned to local needs and aspirations.

Most of the good work we appreciate or think of now has already been done by some civil servant.

Here are ten award-winning initiatives shortlisted by me on the basis of greater public good. The details of the award scheme and projects/initiatives mentioned are sourced from the website of Ministry of Personnel, Public Grievances and

Pensions. The designation of the concerned officer(s) who were part of the award-winning initiatives is at the time of announcement of the awards.

> **Tracking Delhi Government School System**
> Steps were taken to place online information pertaining to attendance of the teachers, marksheets of students, tracking the performance of the students subject-wise, along with information pertaining to various government schools, their location, courses, maps, acts and rules, tenders and circulars etc.
> Evaluation of teachers was introduced based on performance. The system helped in identifying gaps and designing solutions for improvement.
> A very educative and attractive multimedia kit was developed and installed in all schools for the bridge course to help students joining the government schools in Class VI and Class X.
> As a result, the number of government schools with 100% pass-percentage had gone up from 6 in the year 2004-05 to 41 in the year 2006-07 for Class X, and for Class XII from 18 in the year 2004-05 to 46 in the year 2006-07.
> The number of students passing their Class X from government schools increased by 79%, from 41,056 in the year 2005 to 73,497 in the year 2007. This initiative improved the quality of education in the Government schools in NCT of Delhi.

Rajendra Kumar (IAS), Vijay Kumar (IAS), Gitanjali G Kundra (IAS) and Ashok Kumar were awarded for this on April 21, 2008.

Had this pace continued and been regularly modified,

the outcome in the form of quality of education imparted in government owned schools in Delhi and in other parts of the country would have improved drastically.

The condition of government run schools is still not up to the mark.

Governments are now applying most of the initiatives in the schools under their control. Somebody from the government should have ensured that this initiative could have been implemented almost in all parts of the country, irrespective of political differences.

The implementation of this initiative in other parts of the country would have brought praise worthy changes in school education and helped students from not so financially sound backgrounds to do wonders. All these would have led to *'Atmanirbhar Bharat'* or self-reliant India.

E-registration of properties in Bihar

The conventional system of property registration in Bihar was marked by cumbersome procedures, delays and corruption.

Registration was very tedious and time consuming. The system of manually copying deeds in registers had collapsed. The backlog of record maintenance was about 7 to 8 years.

The Registration Department of the Bihar Government wanted to bring in efficiency and transparency in the registration process and restore the confidence of stakeholders.

To meet their expectations, an innovative Information Communication Technology (ICT) based complete solution for e-registration of properties in the state named BiSCORE (Bihar System of Computerized

Registration), was designed and implemented.

It involves complete automation of processes with less paper and state-of-art record archival system at all registry offices of the state.

All 105 registry offices of the state of Bihar were SCORE enabled in a record time of just three months with a cost-effective Hardware on Hire Basis (HOHB) model.

This resulted in increase in the state revenue, accrual of funds in BiSCORE society and created new job opportunities, and a healthy competition amongst entrepreneurs.

BiSCORE demonstrated the innovative use of state-of-art technologies like finger print biometric devices, web camera, scanners, etc.

The entire scheme is self-sustainable and verifiable. It has been completely adapted during 2008 to the age old government working environment and has effectively changed the 200-year old system of manual property registration in the state.

Anil Kumar (IAS), Dilip Kumar (AIG Registration), Birendra Kumar Singh, Baruna Nandan Singh, Nirmal Kishor Prasad, and Sanjay Kumar were honoured on April 21, 2009.

Property registration offices across the country (barring exception that might exist somewhere) are riddled with deep rooted systemic corruption. Why do most of the registration offices of the country not have either this or any advanced technology that completely removes the role of middlemen and any scope of bribery by staff? Is it vested interest or systemic conspiracy to earn extra money?

Implementation of this measure across the country would have revolutionized the property registration offices. It would have also checked corruption in such offices and helped people save their hard earned money that ordinarily goes to corrupt hands at these places.

Making Medicines Affordable in Chittorgarh

The project was initiated to bring down the cost of generic medicines in remote rural villages.

Making quality drugs available at Government Cooperative Medical shops, at less than one-fourth the price at which they are sold in private medical shops, has revolutionized the way drugs and other surgical instruments were procured, disbursed and sold in rural areas within the state of Rajasthan.

The highlight of implementation was ensuring accessibility of drugs, through district wide chain of fair price medicine shops, which serve the OPD and 'Indoor patients' of government hospitals and general public as well.

The initiative included persuasion of doctors to prescribe generic medicines. Procurement of these generic medicines was done as advised by a team of doctors. Certain very prestigious pharmaceutical companies were empanelled as drug procurement partners.

Medicines thus obtained were dispensed through government controlled medical stores, at prices much below MRP (at one-fourth price) and yet making 20% profit, thus making the initiative self-sustainable.

The initiative reached out to the poor (BPL families), preventing them from falling into a debt trap on account of medical expenses.

Affordability of medicines helped them to willingly seek medical treatment.

The award was given to Dr Samit Sharma (IAS), then District

Magistrate, Chittorgarh, Rajasthan on April 21, 2010.

People belonging to the middle-class especially find it difficult to afford quality healthcare services in the country. The plight of poor and marginalized people is unthinkable and known to all.

The coronavirus pandemic has exposed the dying state of health infrastructure, which is on ventilator in most parts of India. The project, had it been implemented across the country, could have brought relief to a large number of people in reducing their medical treatment bills and ensuring *'Ayushman Bharat'*.

River Linking Project in Jalgaon

In 2005, Jalgaon district had received scant rainfall while most of Maharashtra was experiencing flood-like situation.

All water reservoirs were empty and groundwater level was depleting, while in the neighbouring Nasik district, the Girna dam was overflowing.

The Jalgaon district administration implemented an innovative river linking project to divert the excess water from the Girna dam to the water scarce regions of Jalgaon.

Cooperation and support were garnered from all stakeholders to achieve a common objective, viz. tackling water scarcity and providing water for irrigation and other purposes.

The landowners affected by the project became willing partners, as giving away with a part of their land would allow the remaining part of the land to be arable on account of availability of water for irrigation.

The initiative gainfully utilized the excess water from

surplus regions to the water deficit region of Jalgaon.
Thus, it solved the drinking water problem for a population of about 0.85 million in one municipal corporation, five municipal councils and 123 villages, saving the money spent on supply of water by tankers.
It had resulted in an additional storage capacity of 4,886 Mcft of water.
Around 700 medium, small dams, village tanks and percolation tanks were filled and more than 16,000 water wells were recharged because of this river connectivity project.
The irrigated area increased from 13,000 hectares in 2005 to 30,000 hectares in 2008.

The award was given to Vijay Singhal (IAS), then Collector & District Magistrate, Jalgaon, Maharashtra in 2010

Rainfall in the country is not evenly distributed and agriculture in India is a gamble with the monsoons.

India's economy and food security is heavily dependent on the agriculture sector, which is dependent on monsoons as a regular source of irrigation.

Most parts of the country either receive excess rainfall or no rain at all. The source of irrigation is hard to be found in some areas. Fast depleting groundwater and contamination of fresh water sources are other reasons of major worry.

For some flood and drought hit areas of the Indian states, this interlinking project, which was done at minimal cost, has the potential to further boost agriculture production, check farmers' suicides and bring prosperity in a region. All these would have helped towards doubling the farmers' income. Painful, many did not find it worthy of emulation.

Forest Rights in Madhya Pradesh

The Scheduled Tribes and Other Traditional Forest Dwellers (Recognition of Forest Rights) Act 2006 was brought into effect on December 31, 2007.

The initiative to implement the Act with the objective to ensure that tribals and traditional forest dwellers receive entitlement to forest resources, and are protected from exploitation by vested interests, was undertaken in January 2008 in Madhya Pradesh.

The Tribal Welfare Department of the State Government, with the help of its Forest Department developed a detailed software called 'Survey of Forest Dwellers', at the instance of a team of officers.

This software helps the 'users' in entering the data of each beneficiary. The software also gives complete District-wise/Block-wise MIS information.

All information is placed on a website to make the system transparent.

The State Government used the Personal Digital Assistant (PDA), Geographical Information System (GIS) and Global Positioning System (GPS) for digital geo-mapping of land holdings of the claimants.

This facilitated the survey of tribal communities and creation of a database at the district level, making the implementation very efficient and expeditious at a very low cost.

As on March 31, 2009, the State Government received 3,29,184 claims. It had disposed of 13,060 claims and 32,419 title deeds were ready for distribution.

The manner in which the Central Act was implemented made it very cost effective, saving substantial funds to the state government.

The government's successful efforts to reach out to the illiterate tribal population in sensitizing and intending to regularize the forest land occupied by them are evidenced by the large number of applications. Such large scale implementation was achieved without any complaints from any quarter.

OP Rawat (IAS), Jaideep Govind (IAS), Anil Oberoi (IFoS), Rashmi Arun Shami (IAS) and Ashok Kumar Upadhyay, Additional Director were given the PM's award on April 21, 2010.

Most of the people know that the country's mineral resources are found in tribal dominated areas. These areas add to the country's growth but suffer from lack of development.

This unique project had (still has) the potential to solve most problems of forest dwellers and reduce to zero the instances of armed conflicts (including naxalism), protests and other such opposition by tribals in all the naxal-hit states.

The implementation of this project would have helped in ensuring equitable growth of the country's tribal areas through economic development.

Transforming India Post

'Project Arrow' was launched in April 2008 as an innovative integrated approach to reform *India Post* and enhance the quality of services and improve people's experience of select post offices around the country. During Phase-1, 50 post offices were selected and 450 were covered in Phase-2 ending in December 2008. Phase-3, covering 500 post offices is in progress. Innovations include integrated approach to improving technology, processes, and aesthetics related to four areas: mail delivery, savings bank, remittances, and service levels through streamlining and digitization of processes and monitoring and supervision systems that involve stakeholders.

Innovations to improve the 'look and feel' of the post offices include inputs into human resources, branding, technology, and infrastructure.

The objective of this project was to provide all e-enabled services so that post offices become a 'Window to the World' for the *Aam Aadmi*.

IT enabled reliable tools were used to ensure that all postal operations are carried out smoothly and less time is consumed in back end operations.

A Blue Book, which documented What Is To Be Done was brought out wherein all the best practices were summarized. Monitoring performance against Key Performance Indicators (KPIs) is the key to the success of 'Project Arrow'.

The 'Project Arrow' experience is a working model for bringing integrated improvement in the post offices so that customers can feel the difference. External audit of 50 post offices chosen for the pilot revealed 99% improvement in registered letter performance, 94-100% for ordinary mail, 89-99% for speed post, and 100% for money orders.

The award was given to the Ministry of Communication and Information Technology on April 21, 2010.

Common people still face problems while dealing with officials at some post offices – call it their workload or technological handicap, but the problems of non-cooperation still persist.

Generally, people prefer private couriers over Indian postal services. The reason is not because the private courier services are cheap but the ease of convenience.

Projects like this and their improved versions, have the potential to give a tough fight to private courier companies and enhance people's/customer's satisfaction which takes away a major pie of business from the Indian postal department.

24×7 water supply scheme in Satara

Malkapur town (under Buldhana district of Maharashtra) piped water supply scheme, commissioned in 1988 was envisaged to supply 40 liters per capita per day (LPCD) on the basis of an estimated population growth of 14,000 by 2010.

But the town's population increased 50% more than the estimated growth and 10 years earlier than the projection.

This resulted in poor and unreliable supply of water and untimely service. To overcome this problem, a distribution network was designed using the 'Water Gems' software ensuring '24x7 availability' of water.

The transparent process of manufacture of pipes involving the village *Panchayat* members ensured quality.

The methodology regarding the resin to be used for manufacturing these pipes was tendered and accredited by an international agency.

Third party inspection, an essential pre-requisite as per the tender, was carried out and certified by an inspection agency.

Thus, it was ensured that the pipes used for connections conformed to relevant ISO standards. Similarly, Automatic Meter Readers (AMR meters) used in the project too were third party inspected.

Laying of pipelines was properly planned, and phased zone-wise execution was completed well in time.

Local residents and stakeholders, including the public representatives, undertook a special drive to convince people to fix proper stop cocks.

Progressive/telescopic water tariff system was introduced

to curb excessive usage of water.

This initiative improved the delivery time and services of water supply. It also contributed to good quality of water delivery as a result of pressurized water throughout the day and night.

A healthy 30% reduction in wastage of water was ensured with telescopic tariff structure and gradual decrease in the number of hours of water supply from 19-20 hours to 13-14 hours per day.

Simplification of the billing procedure with AMR type meter installation ensured that reading could be taken remotely by driving through the streets using radio frequency driven handheld devices.

As the pumping of water to the water tank on terraces was not required, use of electricity was remarkably reduced leading to energy conservation and reduction in pollution, to an estimated extent of 450 tons of carbon dioxide in the atmosphere.

The system of automation using GSM technology reduced the cost of operation and eliminated the requirement of pump operators.

Rajendra Ganeshlal Holani, Sadanad Kashinath Bhopale, Sunil Yashwant Basugade and Uttam Pandurang Bagade were awarded on April 21, 2011.

Big cities of the country still face water woes for various reasons. Migration and fast drying sources of water add to these woes.

Bursting of water supply pipes, leakages and digging of roads to repair such pipes are common in most cities and towns of the country.

Safe drinking water supply doesn't reach most parts of the country. People travel miles to fetch drinking water.

The project, if implemented, has the potential to ensure long term water availability especially to people living in water scarce areas.

Evacuation of Indians amid civil war in Libya

Libya was engulfed in civil war and was facing severe air strikes from European countries in 2011 following an uprising against their leader, Col Gaddafi.

In the midst of this sudden development that spread like wild fire in Libya and its neighbouring countries like Tunisia and Egypt, the then Ambassador of India in Libya arranged the evacuation of more than 16,000 Indian nationals stranded in Libya in the midst of active full scale war.

Indians were spread across Libya including the hot war zones of Benghazi, Tripoli etc.

Evacuation was organized in a quick and efficient manner by different modes of transport - by air, sea and road to neighbouring countries.

The then Ambassador provided leadership, strategized the evacuation, prepared contingency plans, coordinated with the Indian Government, arranged local logistics, arranged money, streamlined procedures where required and was present on the ground in the hot zones to boost the morale of the staff and stranded Indians.

The evacuation involved a multi-pronged approach.

The Ambassador actively engaged with the then Libyan Government to get vital information about war developments like exit routes etc. besides establishing liaison with various Indian Missions in the neighbourhood of Libya for emergency assistance.

She also made efforts to spread awareness amongst the Indians stranded in Libya to abstain from taking any sides in the civil war.

Arrangements were also made to enable Indians to make calls back home. The then Ambassador could also foresee that most Indians coming out of the active war zones would not be carrying travel documents, therefore, arrangements for 10,000 emergency passports from the Ministry of External Affairs (MEA) were also made, in anticipation.

It was ensured that food and water and other essentials were stocked in the final evacuation centers.

A database of Indians in Libyan cities was prepared to arrange for evacuation by air, sea and also land routes.

There was no loss of Indian life in the planned evacuation. Some Nepalis, Bangladeshis and Filipinos were also evacuated.

India was the only country other than South Korea that was allowed to evacuate its nationals by sea.

An Indian naval ship INS Jalashwa was allowed to dock in a Libyan port amidst heavy fighting to evacuate stranded Indians.

The award was given to Ms M Manimekalai (IFS), the then Ambassador of India to Libya on April 21, 2012.

India's External Affairs Ministry did a superb job during the stewardship of former External Affairs Minister Late Sushma Swaraj. One tweet to her or her ministry brought solutions to the problems faced by Indians abroad.

Diplomats and civil servants have the capability to do good for the people and for the country. Their acts of valour often go unnoticed. They work silently but diligently.

Such instances help India earn more respect from the global community. The evacuation of Nepalis, Bangladeshis and Filipinos reflected India's resolve towards helping the global community.

Educational Initiatives in Dantewada

South Bastar and Dantewada are known for incidences of Naxalism and consequent violence. As a result, children drop out of school and the literacy rate is currently as low as 33 per cent.

The only way to contain extremism is to prevent future generations from following this ideology based on murders.

With this in view, the then District Collector embarked on a mission of mental transformation.

Assessment of *Panchayats* was done with the help of locals, in places which were shut down due to conflicts or destroyed by extremists.

Educated and unemployed local boys and girls were employed as volunteers (*Anudeshaks*) to survey the dropout children and enroll them in pre-fabricated structures.

Incentives were given to these volunteers for every enrolment.

In cases where permanent structures were not possible, the district administration had installed pre-fabricated structures certified by the National Bamboo Mission.

Education was made interesting to attract children and their parents, so that children even from far off places could attend.

Activities like Children Talent Festival, summer camps etc. provided children with a platform to showcase and express their talent.

In Dantewada out of 38,000 students (from Classes I to VII), only 5,116 make it to Classes IX to XII.

To address the problem, clusters from important junctions were chosen to provide residential support.

Thus, it increased the enrolment numbers and also improved the quality of education.

The district administration had also established a

township of 97 acres at a cost of Rs 100 crore, dedicated exclusively for residential and classroom educational facilities.

To add value to those students who had no basic literacy levels, a livelihood college was established on a public private partnership model.

The beneficiaries realized the quantitative and qualitative change in the education system prevailing in the district.

The award was given to Om Prakash Choudhary (IAS), then Collector, Dantewada, Chhattisgarh on April 21, 2013.

Good and affordable education is like a dream for many in most parts of the country. The condition of the education sector is grim especially in remote areas.

This project helped in providing education to people living in the most severe Naxal affected areas of the country.

Naxals would, even currently they do, destroy school buildings and threaten villagers from sending their children to school, thus ensuring their ideology sustains. This project showcases that civil servants can bring education to any part of the country, despite the hostile environment, provided they have the will and vision.

Imagine the transformation of schools and education in the country had this project been implemented by other civil servants/government employees facing similar circumstances in the area they work in.

Rationalising affidavits to reform public service delivery system in Punjab

The project aims at rationalization of affidavits for reforming public service delivery. Affidavits are required in support of facts given by applicants for issue of various certificates, (residence proof etc.).

Affidavits are affirmations by the applicants (supported in some cases by third parties).

Affidavits require stamp paper/stamp fee and need to be sworn before a magistrate or a public notary. Affidavits impose their own cost on the citizens which include buying stamp paper, locating a deed writer, payment to the notary for attestation and of course, the time and effort consumed.

On the other hand, affidavits have no particular sanctity in law and the same function can easily be performed by declarations.

In Punjab alone, it was estimated then that at least half the households file affidavits annually for one service or the other.

Extrapolating this figure to India, the total number may be more than 20 crore citizens/affidavits. Assuming a cost of Rs 400 per affidavit (one day's wage plus stamps, fees and charges), the total expenses incurred by the citizens of India could well be to the extent of Rs 8,000 crore approximately, according to the award citation.

This initiative was implemented in home, SC/BC welfare, agriculture, food and civil supplies, social security, land and records, water supply, health and local government, personnel certificates and police departments.

An analysis of the different department's services, where affidavits were required, was done and discussion was held to review the requirement of affidavits for services of their departments.

Selection of those services where affidavits can be replaced with self declarations was done.

The initiative brought many impacts including improvement in delivery time of services and simplified procedures.

The award was given to The Department of Governance Reforms of the Punjab government on April 21, 2015.

People still face problems in getting an affidavit for a wide variety of works. This can be replaced with self declarations or other such procedures which are hassle free and less time consuming.

The Government of India has done away with the requirement of affidavits in a majority of works and replaced it with self declarations. States need to implement initiatives like this in letter and spirit to improve governance and stem corruption.

There should not be a need for any affidavit and all such requirements should be replaced with self declarations. One who has to lie will do so under oath as well.

Governments have come and gone but the good work done by the officers has always stayed. These aforesaid initiatives got recognition from the Prime Ministers of India as they were out-of-the-box good governance ideas.

It is not that only an officer is recognized through these awards but his colleagues, subordinates and all employees working with him are also appreciated. No officer can unilaterally lead an award winning initiative without the help of all categories of employees working under his or her charge.

There is good work being done by employees at all levels across the country. This work needs to be appreciated and publicized.

Concentrated efforts need to be made to ensure that the projects/initiatives awarded under the PM's awards scheme are emulated in other parts of the country.

How about forming a taskforce with public private partnership to explore ways to seek implementation of these and so many other good governance initiatives implemented by government officials across the country?

Innovation needs to be encouraged among civil servants and may be made a criterion for them to get career progression like empanelments, promotions and foreign postings, among others in their jobs.

Special incentives can also be planned by the government to ensure that good governance ideas get focused attention.

Such encouragement should not be limited to civil servants but kept open for subordinate officers including clerical and support staff as well. This will be a game changer.

My experience reveals that staff at the lower levels of bureaucracy is equally talented and capable of doing/innovating many good governance initiatives.

It would be refreshing to see more creative ideas coming from government employees to change the face and character of governance, especially in rural areas.

There is no dearth of ideas and resources to implement these changes but a courageous mind is needed to execute them to change the face of governance.

And of course, recognition of good work by a lower level employee working at a *Panchayat* level or in far fetched areas of the country is one of the needs of the hour.

Ongoing Reforms and Good Governance Initiatives

National Recruitment Agency and Common Eligibility Test

The Government in August 2019, decided to set up a National Recruitment Agency (NRA), a multi-agency body, for conducting a Common Eligibility Test (CET) to screen or shortlist candidates for Group B and C (non-technical) posts in different central government organizations.

The NRA will have representatives from the Ministry of Railways, Ministry of Finance/Department of Financial Services, Staff Selection Commission (SSC), Railway Recruitment Boards (RRBs) and Institute of Banking Personnel Selection (IBPS).

The purpose of the NRA is to have 'one nation, one test' for recruitment to a majority of government jobs/departments.

At present, candidates seeking government jobs have to appear for separate examinations conducted by multiple recruiting agencies for various posts, for which similar eligibility conditions have been prescribed.

Candidates have to pay fees to multiple recruiting agencies and also travel long distances for appearing in various examinations. These multiple recruitment examinations are a burden on the candidates, as also on the respective recruitment agencies, involving avoidable/repetitive expenditure, law and order/security related issues and venue related problems.

There is also a notion of corruption attached for recruitment to government jobs.

On an average, 2.5 to 3 crore candidates appear in each of these recruitment examinations.

A CET would enable these candidates to appear once and apply to any or all these recruitment agencies for higher level examinations. This would indeed be a boon to all the candidates.

It is envisioned that the NRA would be a specialist body bringing state-of-the-art technology and best practices to the field of recruitment for the central government.

The salient features of NRA and CET:

- NRA to conduct online CET twice a year
- Registration of applicants, generation of roll number/admit cards, display of marks, merit lists, etc, to be done online
- The CET would be available in a number of languages. This would greatly facilitate people from different parts of the country to take the exam and have an equal opportunity of being selected
- The CET will be based on multiple choice objective type questions
- The CET score of a candidate will be valid for three years
- Every district of the country will have an examination centre, including the 117 aspirational districts. CET

will be conducted at over 1,000 centres. Examination centres in every district of the country would greatly enhance access to candidates located in far flung areas

- It will be a major relief to poor candidates. Presently, candidates have to appear in multiple examinations conducted by multiple agencies. Apart from the examination fees, candidates have to incur additional expenses for travel, boarding, lodging and other such activities. A single examination would reduce the financial burden on candidates to a large extent
- Women candidates, especially from rural areas face constraints in appearing for multiple examinations as they have to arrange for transportation and places to stay when exam centres are far away. They sometimes also have to find suitable persons to accompany them to these centres that are located far away. The location of test centres in every district would greatly benefit candidates from rural areas in general and women candidates in particular
- No restriction on the number of attempts by the candidate, subject to the prescribed upper age limit
- Relaxation in upper age limit to be given to candidates of SC/ST/OBC/PwD, etc
- Candidates would have the facility of registering on a common portal and give a choice of centres. Based on availability, they would be allotted centres. The ultimate aim is to reach a stage wherein candidates can schedule their own tests at centres of their choice
- NRA to ensure better access to rural, underprivileged candidates and women

- NRA will facilitate employment generation
- CET scores can be shared with central government, state governments, union territories, public sector undertakings and private sector
- NRA shall conduct a separate CET for each of the three levels – graduate, higher secondary (12th pass) and matriculate (10th pass) candidates, for those non-technical posts to which recruitment is presently carried out by the Staff Selection Commission (SSC), the Railway Recruitment Boards (RRBs) and by the Institute of Banking Personnel Selection (IBPS)
- Based on the screening done at the CET score level, final selection for recruitment shall be made through separate specialized Tiers (II, III etc) of examination which shall be conducted by the respective recruitment agencies
- The curriculum for this test would be common as would be the standard. This would greatly ease the burden of candidates who are at present required to prepare for each of the examinations separately as per different curriculum
- The Government has sanctioned a sum of Rs 1,517.57 crore for the NRA. The expenditure will be undertaken over a period of three years. Apart from setting up the NRA, costs will be incurred for setting up examination infrastructure in the 117 aspirational districts*

* The information is based on the Government of India's press statement and news stories done on the subject by the author.

Mission Karmayogi

The Union Cabinet had in September 2020 approved 'Mission *Karmayogi*',* dubbed as the biggest bureaucratic reform initiative, aimed at capacity building ending the culture of working in silos and ensuring transparency.

The programme will 'radically' improve the government's human resource management practices and prepare civil servants for the future, said Prime Minister Narendra Modi.

The programme will help in overcoming existing impediments like 'lack of lifelong & continuous learning environment', 'evolution of silos at department level preventing shared understanding of India's development aspirations' and 'diverse and fragmented training landscape', among others.

The core guiding principles of the competency driven programme will be to support the transition from 'rules based to roles based' HR management.

To cover around 46 lakh central employees, a sum of Rs 510.86 crore will be spent over five years from 2020-21 to 2024-25 under Mission *Karmayogi* or the National Programme for Civil Services Capacity Building (NPCSCB).

Under Mission *Karmayogi*, the appointing authorities will have ready-made data for choosing 'the right candidate for the right job'. There is a provision for real time evaluation in ensuring accountability and transparency in governance.

Mission *Karmayogi* aims to prepare Indian civil servants for the future by making them more creative, constructive,

* The details on Mission Karmayogi are based on the press statement issued by the Government of India and a story done by the author based on the subject.

imaginative, innovative, proactive, professional, progressive, energetic, enabling, transparent and technology enabled.

It will build future-ready civil service with the right attitude, skills and knowledge, aligned to the vision of new India.

The programme envisages use of Artificial Intelligence (AI) in assigning official roles to the civil servants besides assessing their work.

A Public Human Resources Council comprising of select Union Ministers, Chief Ministers, eminent public HR practitioners, thinkers, global thought leaders and public service functionaries under the chairmanship of the Prime Minister will serve as the apex body for providing strategic direction to the task of reforming the civil services and its capacity building.

It is also proposed to set up a Capacity Building Commission which will ensure a uniform approach in managing and regulating the capacity building ecosystem on a collaborative and co-sharing basis.

The Commission will also come out with an 'Annual State of Civil Service Report'.

An integrated government online training platform – iGOTKarmayogi – will be set up for the Mission.

iGOTKarmayogi platform will bring scale and state-of-the-art infrastructure to augment the capacities of over two crore officials in India.

For the program, there will be a Special Purpose Vehicle (SPV) for owning and operating the digital assets and technological platform for online training and a coordination unit headed by the Cabinet Secretary.

NPCSCB has been carefully designed to lay the foundations for capacity building for civil servants so that they remain entrenched in Indian culture and sensibilities and remain connected to their roots, while they learn from the best institutions and practices across the world.

The expenditure is partly funded by multilateral assistance to the tune of USD 50 million.

Besides capacity building, service matters like confirmation after probation, deployment, work assignment and notification of vacancies, etc. would eventually be integrated with the proposed competency framework.

Multi Source Feedback Appraisal System

The central government follows a 360 degree appraisal system or Multi Source Feedback* (MSF) system to assess bureaucrats on integrity and reputation, through a comprehensive background check, before their empanelment or for appointing them at senior levels.

The system, which is said (as there is no official order on it yet) to be brought into practice in 2015, is dictated by the mantra of 'right person for the right job' and claims to have ended lobbying for different coveted posts.

Before this system, empanelment to the posts of Joint Secretary and above in the government was done by an experts panel that would scrutinise the marks of the annual performance appraisal reports of the officer for the past 10 years and aggregate the scores for every year.

This had led to a situation where most officers were graded

---

* The details are based on the Personnel Ministry's official documents, Parliamentary Panel's report of August 2017 and stories done on the subject by the author.

as outstanding without any differentiation on the basis of specific aspects of their performance and character.

However, a Parliamentary Committee has said that the 360 degree appraisal system needs to be made more transparent and rule based.

The committee noted the concerns raised by various stakeholders that the empanelment under the Central Staffing Scheme is not providing a level playing field to all participating services, especially the non-IAS services.

All institutions or bodies involved in the empanelment and appointment process of Joint Secretary and above level posts under the Government of India predominantly comprises officers of only one service, the IAS, the Department Related Parliamentary Standing Committee on Personnel, Public Grievances, Law and Justice had said in its report tabled in Parliament in August 2017.

"This is perceived by non-IAS services to have tilted the balance in favor of the IAS in the empanelment and placement process," it had said.

A system needs to be put in place for deciding on promotion of all categories of officers, be it support staff or senior clerks.

They need to be periodically assessed using this and other methods to keep deadwood and work shirkers away from the governance system.

Clean India Mission

It is a praise worthy effort by the Government of India. It has brought many changes across the country. Ever since its launch on October 2, 2014, the '*Swachh Bharat*' or 'Clean India' mission has become a national movement.

On one hand it has made people aware of cleanliness and its impact, nationally and internationally, on the country and its image. On the other hand, it has proved that civil servants can deliver and act swiftly on the Prime Minister's call.

The Clean India Mission – further divided into urban and rural categories – is aimed at making urban India free from open defecation and achieving 100 per cent scientific management of municipal solid waste in over 4,000 statutory towns in the country, according to the Ministry of Housing and Urban Affairs.

The objectives of the mission are also eradication of manual scavenging, to effect behavioural change regarding healthy sanitation practices and generate awareness about sanitation and its linkage with public health.

The Government of India periodically does a cleanliness survey to assess the progress made by different towns/cities/ municipalities on different parameters. Its findings are then made public.

This mission has brought significant changes in the country, in people's behaviour and in waste management.

However, people need to do more to ensure that the movement meets its desired objective.

The key to achieve that is change in public behaviour. People need to be extra vigilant and ensure that they dispose garbage at designated places/bins.

With regard to bureaucracy, the concerned officers need to take a lead and ensure that the office premises under their jurisdiction are free from any kind of garbage and junk, such as used furniture or construction material.

The government may also consider an annual survey

to identify and award a clean office premise and the officer concerned for doing it.

Those lagging should also be named so that they may improve.

This suggested ranking system, if accepted and implemented, can bring drastic changes in government offices across the country, which often wear dilapidated looks and sport stains of *Pan Masala* etc.

15-Sutras for Good Governance

I have raised the view points of the common man in this book. Majority of people of this country feel that they are still the victims of insensitivity and apathy of an inefficient governance system manned by largely intelligent and sensitive civil servants.

Governance is not only about ensuring corruption free and hassle free access to public facilities, utilities and infrastructure, but is also about creating a positive image of the country at the global level and above all ensuring ease of good governance.

Why should government jobs be considered by some as a means to earn quick money and lead an easy life with no accountability?

Why should India not be seen as a model of good governance worldwide? After all, we have highly professional civil servants and a decisive and mature political leadership.

However, there exists a strong perception of inefficiency, corruption, red-tape and unprofessional governance system in the minds of many people not only in the country but across the world.

It can be argued that these are legacy issues but that still places the onus on everyone to rectify these issues for the larger good of the country.

This is when many Indians, including some retired bureaucrats and private individuals, are behind development/part of development of a good governance system in most of the countries.

But why do they fail in developing such foolproof governance system in India where common people are not exploited, business community is encouraged and corruption is swiftly and sternly punished?

Big governance reforms have been frequently announced by the governments. But, all of them have failed in changing the face of governance – a clean and efficient working system where people feel happy and satisfied in approaching public authorities instead of having a fear of harassment or facing unprofessional behavior from the employees working in these departments.

Based on my trysts with the country's bureaucracy, here are *15-sutras* for ensuring a sustainable state of governance that may help people and the country the most.

These are not big ticket reforms that will require governments to bring about major regulatory changes. Most of these suggested changes can be brought in by individuals concerned, i.e. the employees. In some cases, they require intervention/guidance from seniors or heads of the departments.

The suggested reforms have the potential of changing the face and character of the mysterious '*Babudom*' that the common man is afraid of.

Deputation of armed forces personnel

Though many civil servants outright reject it but I strongly feel that the government may consider bringing on deputation or on fixed term basis, eligible and willing officials from the defence forces – the Army, Navy and Air Force – and from central armed police forces, like the Central Reserve Police Force (CRPF), National Security Guard (NSG), Border Security Force (BSF) among others, to man posts in civil ministries like road transport, commerce, culture and personnel.

Officers in the defence and armed services possess and practice all office work that might be handled by civil servants in ensuring administration of any other central government department/organization.

They can also be posted at suitable posts in municipal councils and corporations besides Regional Transport Offices (RTOs) and excise department, as a test case under the jurisdiction of the state governments.

This suggestion, I feel, has the potential to check corruption, red tapism and tardiness in government offices.

This measure will also help in increasing inter services bonhomie among civil and defence personnel.

Imagine what kind of reform this measure may bring considering the kind of respect and discipline the armed forces personnel follow while performing their duty in defending the country's frontiers. Not that hard to try in a department.

Four uniformed officers were in May 2021 appointed as Additional Secretary and Joint Secretaries in the Department of Military Affairs under the Defence Ministry by the Government of India.

Training of lower and mid-level workforce

There exists a policy framework to train civil servants and certain senior level employees at regular intervals. However, there is

expected by all – be it the policy makers or the people at large.

There is a need to ensure strict adherence to Government of India's policy of zero tolerance towards corruption or corrupt practices.

An example can be drawn from Singapore, whose founding father Lee Kuan Yew made Singapore what it is today. How he ensured that civil servants observe the highest degree of integrity and promoted efficient governance is known to all and is a model lesson for all those interested in public administration.

There is a need to ensure that corruption hit departments are taken up by the governments concerned for the clean up process. For instance, the work culture at the Regional Transport Offices (RTOs), municipal corporations and revenue offices, among others needs to be changed.

Those incharge of these departments must ensure that people are not fleeced by the employees working there. Systemic corruption from such departments must be eliminated. The governments may come up with awards and rewards to encourage employees for achieving zero corruption.

How about a special reward scheme for somebody who makes a unit, section, division, wing or an organization corruption free?

Nomination based appointment of experts

The Government of India has taken a courageous measure to allow lateral entry – experts from private sector in the government – and it is expected to bring in the desired results.

There is a provision for nomination of a person of eminence from the fields of sports, arts and media among others in the Upper House of the Parliament, the Rajya Sabha.

We have seen sports persons, journalists and others from different fields being nominated. Why can't the same system be implemented in bureaucracy? Why can't a talented resource from the private sector be appointed in the central government for a fixed tenure with a designated task of achieving a governance goal?

Why cannot a telecom sector expert from a private company be a part of the Telecom Ministry? Similarly, a sports person can be made part of the Sports Ministry or an educationist of the Education Ministry or a journalist of the Information and Broadcasting Ministry and so on.

The government needs to open its doors for such experts to bring the desired changes in the country's administrative system but with caution. Such appointments must be fair and free from nepotism and favouritism.

The government may also consider having more services like the Indian Teaching Service or Indian Agriculture Service among others to bridge the gap that exists in education and agriculture sectors.

Model village offices

It is said that India lives in its villages. It is by and large assumed that governance at the Centre is comparatively better than that in the states. However, there are more subjects related to people's welfare in the state's domain than in the Centre.

Be it matters related to law and order, water and electricity supply, registration of property, housing boards, roads, permission needed for starting businesses, etc., most of these are of daily concern to the common citizen and these are vested with the local government or authorities.

I have personal experience and can vouch for the effectiveness of its redressal mechanism. The only thing that can be done to make it better is to ensure 100 per cent resolution of grievances raised on this platform, that too, in the quickest time possible.

State governments must have a system like CPGRAMS for all its departments including those working at village or town levels. It will be a real game changer in ensuring clean and efficient administration.

There must be strict monitoring of successful and satisfactory (though it may be subjective) resolution of such online grievances as well.

Doors of government offices, especially those in rural areas, must be opened wide for common people. Government employees, by default, appear to be maintaining distance from the common man, may be due to paucity of time or owing to their hectic schedules. Efforts must be made to ensure that people get hassle free access to governance or public service delivery.

There can also be a single website to file grievances related to any of the government authorities under the central and state governments.

Easy tracking of complaints filed on such online platforms with time bound resolution would bring unimaginative reforms in governance.

Proper implementation of minimum tenure policy

There are instances in public domain regarding deviation from implementation of the Government of India's minimum tenure policy for bureaucrats aimed at checking political interference or witch hunting by vested interests.

On the contrary, there are officers in different services and departments who have never worked outside Delhi for most of their career, thanks to their contacts.

Frequent transfers and postings discourage an employee from giving his 100 per cent to the job. It also affects his morale. There has to be a foolproof, may be judicial oversight (as the minimum tenure policy was formed after a directive of the Supreme Court) to ensure that there is no deviation by any government department from executing the minimum tenure policy, which in most cases is two years for an officer at a particular post.

There is also a need to routinely post lower and middle level staff, from peons to senior clerks in different departments, in a way that it doesn't cause hardship to the employees and people at large. Those found possessing special abilities and traits to perform a particular task should be encouraged and given a chance to do so.

Such periodical transfers will fill these employees with fresh energy to perform and transform.

A minimum tenure policy needs to be implemented in letter and spirit in the central and state governments. Some of the state governments are infamous for carrying out massive reshuffle of employees for reasons well known to all of us.

Similarly, employees need to be moved to other departments/ wings through the rotational transfer policy to keep corruption and inefficiency at bay. Such rotational transfers would also help an employee gain different experiences and break the monotony of the work that might emerge while working at a place or in a department for long.

The policy of rotational transfer of people working at sensitive posts – prone to corruption – has to be implemented effectively.

United Kingdom by the conservative government of John Major in 1991 as a national programme with a simple aim: to continuously improve the quality of public services for the people of the country so that these services respond to the needs and wishes of the users.

The state and central governments should ensure that all its departments mandatorily display the Citizens' Charters in all its offices, in both physical and digital form, in English, Hindi and regional languages to help the local people. This initiative is especially desired at village level, in *panchayats* and in other remote areas of the country.

It has the potential to improve local level governance.

Protection from political changes

Bureaucracy should be free from any impact of government change. The larger cause of people and the country's welfare should be of paramount priority for any government which is in power.

There are frequent elections and change in governments in our country (until one nation one election is implemented). For instance, a project, irrespective of it being good, envisaged by 'Government-A' in power is nixed by the 'Government-B' that came into helm after winning the elections.

This acts as a setback for many.

Political changes in an area should not have any adverse effect on the bureaucracy. The executive must be left free from the clutches of political masters to work efficiently and effectively.

Rules should be a government employee's best friend. A government employee can perform efficiently if he is well versed with the rules and official procedures.

Most government employees are introduced to the rules at the time of joining the service.

There is no refresher course in between for these government employees, except for the civil servants who attend career trainings at regular intervals.

There is a need to devise a procedure to ensure that all employees are well versed with the rules needed to perform any assigned task.

Revamp government offices

Taking a cue from the Clean India Mission, which is very close to my heart, I would suggest that government offices should be revamped and made free from all clutter.

There also has to be a provision for clean toilets in government offices, especially those at village, town and district levels, as people, mainly women, avoid visiting these places fearing that the long wait (which one has to usually face to meet an officer) would be problematic for them.

Most of the government offices, especially in the states and that too in rural areas, do not even have provisions for drinking water. In a tropical country like ours, this is a basic necessity as it compounds the problems of a long agonizing wait along with problems associated with dehydration.

The condition of government offices in rural areas is pathetic and they are badly in need of renovation.

Stains of *Pan Masala* and junk like unwanted furniture and construction material lying in the government premises is a common sight in most parts of the country. Central government offices are also no exception to such common sight of garbage that can be disposed easily.

every such thing built by tax payers money, which is ultimately the money of the people and for the people.

It is the tax payers' money, popularly known as the government money, which is spent on creating public infrastructures to make our life easier and convenient.

I would rather not say that some people lack civic sense, either by choice (ignorance/insensitivity and careless attitude) or by compulsion (poverty/lack of privilege). But people need to value the government infrastructure, appreciate the good work and question the authorities concerned in case they spot deficiencies. If we start doing so, the change will then be visible to all of us.

Let us all try and become responsible citizens, in whatever work we do, and contribute towards the betterment of the society before we crib about the *babudom* or find fault with the way we are governed!

Most people are also not aware of the fundamental duties of every citizen of this great country.

As per the constitution, it shall be the duty of every citizen of India –

(a) To abide by the Constitution and respect its ideals and institutions, the National Flag and the National Anthem;

(b) To cherish and follow the noble ideals which inspired our national struggle for freedom;

(c) To uphold and protect the sovereignty, unity and integrity of India;

(d) To defend the country and render national service when called upon to do so;

(e) To promote harmony and spirit of common brotherhood

amongst all the people of India transcending religious, linguistic and regional or sectional diversities; to renounce practices derogatory to the dignity of women;

(f) To value and preserve the rich heritage of our composite culture;

(g) To protect and improve the natural environment including forests, lakes, rivers and wild life, and to have compassion for living creatures;

(h) To develop the scientific temper, humanism and the spirit of inquiry and reform;

(i) To safeguard public property and to abjure violence;

(j) To strive towards excellence in all spheres of individual and collective activity so that the nation constantly rises to higher levels of endeavour and achievement;

(k) Who is a parent or guardian to provide opportunities for education to his child or, as the case may be, ward between the age of six and fourteen years.

One can safely assume the state of affairs in India will certainly improve if all of us start following these fundamental duties in toto.

I will conclude the writing by saying that 'honesty begets honesty, in public and personal life'.

My writing in this book mainly reflects the views of the common man who like me aspires to see this vivid bureaucracy rise to the level of excellence and showcase a world class model of good governance that we all can be proud of. I don't feel this is too much to ask for? Isn't it?

हो गई है पीर पर्वत-सी पिघलनी चाहिए,
इस हिमालय से कोई गंगा निकलनी चाहिए।

आज यह दीवार, परदों की तरह हिलने लगी,
शर्त लेकिन थी कि ये बुनियाद हिलनी चाहिए।

हर सड़क पर, हर गली में, हर नगर, हर गाँव में,
हाथ लहराते हुए हर लाश चलनी चाहिए।

सिर्फ हंगामा खड़ा करना मेरा मकसद नहीं,
सारी कोशिश है कि ये सूरत बदलनी चाहिए।

मेरे सीने में नहीं तो तेरे सीने में सही,
हो कहीं भी आग, लेकिन आग जलनी चाहिए।

दुष्यंत कुमार

How I wish a government employee to be?

I am an optimistic person and my thoughts on bringing about changes in bureaucracy are reflection of that optimism.

I would conclude my optimism on bureaucracy with the following wishful characteristics of a government employee – be it central or state governments – which we all wish to experience:

- I wish a government employee is polite, courteous, easy to approach and helpful.
- I wish a government employee is meticulous in his or her work.
- I wish a government employee does not only finish in time his assigned task with utmost dedication and sincerity but also brings creativity to his or her work.
- I wish a government employee never shrugs off work.
- I wish a government employee tries hard to find ways to be helpful to the common people.
- I wish a government employee does not indulge in direct or indirect corruption and does not harbor graft.
- I wish a government employee presents himself/herself as an epitome of the good work done by him/her for public good.
- I wish people could also be the change they wish to see in the world.

I wish…

Annexure

Voices on Bureaucracy

Here are two opinion pieces by subject experts well versed with the bureaucracy. The views expressed in these articles are personal of the writers.

Break the steel frame

Former secretary to the Government of India, Jawhar Sircar had criticized the bureaucracy.

"There is no point in denying that the Indian bureaucracy is one of the worst in the world and is widely notorious for its labyrinthine rules and genetic negativity. India is also among the most corrupt nations; surely a large part of the bureaucracy must have either connived in it or abdicated its tasks," said Sircar in his article on bureaucracy published in The Telegraph on September 14, 2017.

Elected to the Rajya Sabha on 2 August 2021 on an AITC ticket to represent the State of West Bengal, Sircar is a 1975 batch (retired) officer of the Indian Administrative Service (IAS) of West Bengal cadre.

Even John Kerry's quote about the Indian bureaucracy was very well publicized when he said that "India's economy will only be able to maintain its impressive growth if its bureaucracy ceases to be an expert in setting up roadblocks". Kerry had told this to a group of students during his visit to the Indian Institute of Technology (IIT) Delhi, in September 2016. He was then the Secretary of State, USA.

American think tank Carnegie Endowment for International Peace in a study said that, "The IAS of today is hampered by several concomitant issues: a decline in the quality of recruits, political interference, perverse incentives for career advancement, a lack of specialized expertise, and a perception of widespread corruption."

These quotes are sufficient to understand the Indian bureaucracy. It is true that bureaucrats, particularly lower *babus* are found fussier. It is a fact that the Indian bureaucracy is marred by casteism, regionalism, nepotism and all sorts of 'isms' prevalent in the society.

It would not be wrong to say that the Indian bureaucracy lacks internal cohesion. There are many who go to any extent to appease their political masters to secure their future considerations.

In India, the state administration is highly politicized. Instances have been found where officers affiliated with the ruling party are given key posts. When that party loses the election then those officers are given side postings and the new ruling party brings officers of its liking.

They do not hesitate from inviting officers of their liking from other states so that they can rule the state according to their whims. Actually, in the name of voter's mandate, leaders of the ruling parties try to impose the party's agenda.

In such a scenario, even officers of the All India Services face a tough time in dealing with the state machinery. That is the reason many officers of All India Services such as the Indian Administrative Service (IAS), Indian Police Service (IPS) and Indian Forest Service (IFoS) prefer central deputation and spend their maximum time at the Centre.

Complex grudges and frustrations are the salient features of the Indian bureaucracy. The country has about two dozen organized services. Officers for these services are recruited through the Civil Service Examination (CSE) conducted by the UPSC.

These include IAS, IFS, IPS, Indian Information Service (IIS), Indian Revenue Service (IRS), Indian Telecommunication Service (ITS), Indian Postal Service (IPoS) and Indian Audit and Account Service (IA&AS).

If a candidate gets IAS, he will become super boss and develop a superiority complex. Though, the government has a rule for timely promotion for officers of all services. But IAS officers not only get timely promotion but for them rules are also relaxed. For example, an IAS officer becomes Joint Secretary (JS) in the Government of India in 17 years, while for officers of other services it's like a dream.

Many officers become JS after 18 to 24 years. By the time an IAS officer is due for another promotion that of Additional Secretary.

Such anomaly developed grudges against the IAS and frustration in officers of other services. In an organization there are frequent fights between direct recruits (DR) and promotees (PR). This cold war could be seen in states also between the officers of state services and AIS officers (IAS, IPS and IFoS).

In states, the IAS officers are appointed District Magistrates and IPS officers get a chance to become Superintendents of Police (SPs).

DR and PR tension can be seen in almost all the government departments.

The second big reason for dissatisfaction is the qualifying service for the next promotion. Since IAS officers get timely promotion therefore, they fulfill the required qualifying service criteria. For this privilege they become the Heads of Departments (HoD) and can be posted to any department.

Only an IAS officer can go from Sports to Finance, from Culture to Corporate Affairs, from Skill Development to Information & Broadcasting, from Education to Transport, from Social Justice to Mines.

From authorities such as Delhi Development Authority to Doordarshan and All India Radio, a Chief Gazetteer could be posted in the Transport department. Only an IAS officer can go as the Secretary General to Lok Sabha and Rajya Sabha straight from his cadre.

In most cases, a 'special' officer can be posted in places like World Health Organization (WHO), International Monetary Fund (IMF) and Asian Development Bank (ADB). No matter if he has no experience in this specialized function.

Many IAS officers, who are posted at these offices do not have the subject knowledge or are posted for the first time in such highly professional organizations.

Officers of the Indian Foreign Service (IFS) specialize in diplomacy. They are experts in their field. Officers of no other service can replace them from their domain. But they are also not posted to such international organizations.

An IAS officer of science, engineering, humanities or medical background can easily be posted as the Comptroller and Auditor General (CAG) or Governor of the Reserve Bank of India (RBI),whereas officers of IA&AS and Indian Economic Service (IES) are not considered fit for this specialized job.

The Carnegie study has pointed out this shortcoming of the Indian bureaucracy. Though the UPSC selects officers for specialized jobs but they are denied the top job.

Like an IRS officer will not be posted as Revenue Secretary, an IPS officer will not get a chance to be posted as Home Secretary and an IES officer cannot be a Finance Secretary.

Only IPS officers are fit for the Director General's (DGs) post. Cadre service officers will never be considered for such posts. Maximum post retirement jobs also seem to be reserved for the IAS only.

This attitude is causing dissentient among officers of other services.

Politics is also one of the root causes. Politics is deeply rooted in the state machinery and that is the reason despite the Supreme Court's order, not a single state is interested in police reforms which are pending for the last five decades.

According to experts such situation suits them. Many service related government departments are defamed for delaying work unless *babus* get their mandatory cut.

In states merit and seniority is not a criterion. Who will become a particular state's Chief Secretary or DGP will totally depend on the sweet will of the CM and the ruling party.

Even Sub Divisional Magistrates (SDMs) and Station House Officers (SHOs) are appointed on the recommendation of the people's representatives of the area.

When the NDA came into power at the Centre, they also faced many challenges. Even after six years in power the party is still searching for hard working, honest and result oriented officers. That is the reason why about half a dozen officers are holding two to three charges.

The NDA government is also recruiting experts through lateral entry (i.e. private sector specialists) and re-appointing good officers on contract basis.

The government is facing stiff opposition by some fellow officials on this lateral entry.

As per Sircar, "The worrisome question is why do university toppers, who succeed in the Union Public Service Commission examinations, fail to deliver thereafter?

"Either some mysterious force holds them back or we just accept the terrible fact that personal zeal or honesty can hardly change a bottom dominated politicized pyramid".

The Berggruen Governance Index 2019 report ranked India poorly on business regulation, public health and civil justice. The report looked at data over 14 years (2004-2018) from 38 countries and covered 95 per cent of the global GDP and 75 per cent of the global population.

Officers of only three services – IAS, IPS and IFoS have been allotted cadre (state/Union Territory). But the Government of India (GoI) is their cadre controlling authority.

Therefore, states cannot take any action against these officers. They can only recommend. GoI is the final authority. This practice is seen as dual citizenship for these officers.

During the British Raj, Warren Hastings laid the foundation of Civil Services and Charles Cornwallis reformed, modernized, and rationalized it. Hence, Cornwallis is known as the father of Civil Services in India. Cornwallis introduced two divisions of the Indian civil service – covenanted and uncovenanted.

No doubt, the task of cleaning the system is daunting unless the political leadership desires so. But the question is who will take the lead in cleaning the ailing bureaucracy?

Instances have come to light that officers who tried to re-rail the system were transferred. Such action by the government de-motivates a just officer.

It is also very unusual that after seven decades our political leadership could not formulate a good system which suits every citizen of the country. Now the time has come to break the 'steel frame' of bureaucracy and make it public friendly and result oriented.

Ajay Kumar Chaturvedi
Former Indian Information Service Officer

Is there any 'steel' left in the frame?

The recent Transparency International Report has said India has the highest (39%) bribery rate in Asia. Frankly, I was not much surprised or shocked to read that.

Having closely studied a large cross section of the Indian bureaucracy, both from All India Services and others, for over 30 years, I strongly feel that what Sardar Patel had envisioned as the formidable 'steel frame', has almost crumbled after 70 years.

There is hardly any *steel* left in the *frame* which was supposed to prop up the new democratic set-up of India, and in turn, mitigate the plight of the common man to achieve development.

Uncontrollable corruption, lack of efficiency, almost total insulation from any penal action for their omissions and commissions have made government officials, from top to bottom, the butt of severe criticism, as also the cause of cynicism in the eyes of the people.

The so-called highly educated *Babus*, upon their entry into the hallowed precincts of an all-powerful government, ostensibly to serve the people, swiftly change their colours like a chameleon.

They start thinking first for themselves, their families, their children and friends and then come the people. Of course, there are honourable exceptions in the rotten system across India who are holding up good governance practices, whatever is left of it.

A very senior lawyer once told me that half of the huge number of pending cases in different courts of India would not have been there if the concerned administrators had done their job well and in time.

The tendency to keep matters undecided for many years and finally forcing people to knock the court doors for costly justice is sadly increasing among the bureaucrats.

I may be sounding a little frustrated but if you ask any individual who has had an opportunity to deal with a municipal officer or a revenue official or much less, a Station House Officer (SHO: Incharge of a police station) or an engineer in the Central Public Works Department (CPWD) or an irrigation department of any state, you will hear shocking stories of either inordinate delays or heavy extortion of money or gross injustice or perhaps all put together!

Which department's officers are more corrupt than others is anybody's guess. Flip through newspapers and you would see one or the other officer is caught by anti-corruption agency and huge ill gotten wealth is unearthed.

An Arvind Joshi from Madhya Pradesh and a Babulal Agarwal from Chhattisgarh are just the tip of the iceberg of widespread corruption that was seen and proved in recent times. That both officers hailed from the prestigious and premier Indian Administrative Service (IAS) is just a coincidence.

What is rare, however, is that both were adequately punished.

Most others from Indian Police Service (IPS), Indian Revenue Service (IRS) or subordinate services, are not caught by any of the multiple agencies is no reason for us to consider them honest public servants.

Unfortunately, despite several administrative reforms there is no robust inbuilt system, other than Annual Confidential Reports or ACRs (which are generally well managed) to make them accountable for what they have done or what they have not done, in a given role.

Once a new recruit cracks the tough Civil Services Exam, he or she is mostly likely to superannuate from the highest possible level, if age is on their side.

Not all can become the Chief Secretary or the Director General of Police or Head of Forest Forces (HoFF), but regular promotions, pay rise and other perks are almost always guaranteed till the last day of a well protected service.

Whether they perform or not is nobody's concern. Even the society does not collectively rise against this injustice and that is sad.

In Indore, the commercial capital of the central Indian state of Madhya Pradesh, a housing scheme floated by the Indore Development Authority (IDA), headed mostly by IAS officials, is dragging on for more than 35 years and is a case in point, as far as the role of bureaucracy is concerned.

The vexed issue of the Indian bureaucracy's failure to help the common man overcome his problems does not merely relate to economic corruption and misuse of their powers to benefit themselves in any manner, but also to the weak political and societal supervision.

A lot has been written about political corruption in India, but we can't ignore the fact that an elected people's representative, some of them with modest educational backgrounds, has to go back to the people every five years, something the bureaucrats don't have to. They don't have to appear for five-yearly exams like that of an MP or an MLA.

An inept, arrogant and corrupt politician (*panch*, *sarpanch* or Member of Legislative Assembly (MLA) or a Member of Parliament) can be taught a lesson by people at the hustings but that is not possible in case of a well heeled and adequately insulated officer.

Therefore, fixing accountability and ensuring measurable performance of a bureaucrat becomes important in the world's largest bureaucracy.

The Modi government has taken many measures to take bureaucrats to task but still a lot needs to be done to make them responsible and accountable, including premature and forced retirements.

The 360 degrees formula before an important posting, technological interventions to speed up disposal of files, efforts to bring in transparency and lateral entry of private sector professionals are all fine, but unless and until bureaucrats start having empathy for those who come to them for solutions, the man on the street will never be able to smile.

However, I must also hasten to add here that there have also been some extraordinary officers who tried to transform the system on their own and through out-of-box thinking or with courage to take on the system they proved that positive changes are possible.

During the COVID-19 pandemic undoubtedly, the bureaucracy did rise to the occasion and I would like to salute them. But for them the deaths would have been far far more in numbers than what we actually saw.

Elsewhere, there have been officers who took on mighty mining mafia or powerful politicians to favour ordinary people and uphold the law of the land. Such officers are few and far between.

In this connection, I would like to especially praise the forest officials who have almost always stood by nature, forests & wildlife.

I would conclude this piece with a reference to a beautifully written article by an honest officer.

Ms Dipali Rastogi, a Principal Secretary in Madhya Pradesh, had caused a tremor in bureaucracy with her hard hitting article in which she laid bare the myths of the powerful IAS by stating: "We are in the service to serve. The truth is, we scarcely behave as servants; we distribute largesse which does not belong to us and we do work for which we are not trained".

She had ended her small but bold piece by saying.... "If there were any justice, we would have long been extinct. But we are too powerful to let ourselves be annihilated....We are the IAS".

Abhilash Khandekar
Senior journalist

Praise for the Book

Good Governance is best represented by "commitment to larger public good against all odds". India's 21st century governance is represented not only by high moral overtones with a universal dimension, but also marked by digital governance initiatives which have reduced significantly the prolonged interface between the citizens and government, social inclusion and a zero tolerance to corruption.

There is high value attached to leadership skills, fairness and impartiality. Modern-day governance entails complex decision making with significant regulatory oversight.

Governments have endeavoured to improve quality of delivery of services. This is being seen through a number of innovative practices including integrated service portals, digital secretariats and timely redressal of public grievances.

A lot has been written about the challenges of modern day governance and improvements that have been brought about. Ashwini Shrivastava has written a comprehensive book on the relationship between the Government and citizens based on his vast experience as a senior journalist in covering civil servants.

The book is of interest not only to scholars but also to the general public.

V Srinivas
IAS/1989 Batch/Rajasthan cadre
Special Secretary, GOI
Director General, National Centre for Good Governance

Road map

I know Ashwini as an energetic young journalist with sharp insights since I joined Election Commission of India in 2015.

He has embarked on writing about India's Bureaucracy and Governance.

India's bureaucracy has worked wonders under able political leaders of yore and at times not so able ones.

Steel Frame has really served our country well in as much as after 70 years of independence we are still a thriving democracy and we have delivered free and fair elections resulting in bloodless transfer of power every time.

However, peoples' aspirations have been rising and comparisons with other countries at times give the feeling that bureaucracy could have done better.

In this context, Ashwini's book may be interesting to read as an outsider's view on the functioning of the Indian Bureaucracy and Governance.

Hopefully, it may also provide some ways for improving our systems which may be useful for budding administrators and civil service aspirants.

O P Rawat
IAS/1977 Batch/Madhya Pradesh cadre
Former Chief Election Commissioner of India

A Distant Entity

Ashwini Shrivastava is a journalist of repute and has been covering various events, mainly in the government sector for nearly a decade and a half.

I first met him about 10 years back when I was Commissioner of Customs in Delhi and Ashwini would meet me to get news feeds on new developments in my office, and we became friends.

When Ashwini called me a few days ago informing me that he was publishing a book on the Indian bureaucracy which he interestingly titled *Decoding Indian Babudom*. I was pleasantly surprised.

I guessed that his book would have been inspired by his various interactions with government servants across different departments. But when he requested me to write my views on '*babudom*', I suddenly found myself at a loss for words even though I had spent over three decades in '*babudom*'. The dilemma was how as an insider, could I write in an impartial, dispassionate way?

Every organization, big or small, has a 'bureaucracy', a hierarchical administrative set-up to implement the organizations' policies, conduct its day-to-day activities, plan for its future and further its goals.

India's administrative set-up is largely inherited from the British regime at the time of independence. However, when India gained independence after centuries of foreign rule there was a tectonic change in the political ethos and structure.

From being an erstwhile colony of a foreign power which was remotely controlled by political masters sitting in England, India had become a truly democratic country governed by representatives elected by its own people through free and fair elections cutting across class, caste, religion, language, region, gender and so on.

This sea change in the political set-up covered every sphere of governance – from the Union to States right up to the *Panchayats* in the villages.

The *'babus'* implement laws and policies laid down by the political masters. In a democratic polity, the political representatives being directly elected by the citizens represent the will of the public at large. Therefore, the 'bureaucrat' theoretically became a servant of the public, unlike the past when the official was only a representative of the crown.

In the pre-Independence era the government official yielded immense power in the name of the ruler and hence the culture was 'feudal'.

Post independence such powers exercised by officers are mandated to serve the interest of the public and not the ones who are governed.

The administrative organizations post independence were also creatures of the imperial regime of the British. Therefore, in spite of the complete change in the political character of the country, from being a colony of the British crown to an independent, self-governing entity, the Indian bureaucracy perhaps could not quite remodel itself from one where the official was a person exercising power for the benefit of the crown to one which is truly a 'public servant'.

It is perhaps this inability to completely transform itself in true letter and spirit that has contributed to the bureaucracy often being viewed as a distant entity by the public which some would like to view with suspicion or even disdain.

However, to be fair to the Indian bureaucracy, given India's size in terms of its geography, population and diversity, the burden of its long and often cruel history and the enormous challenges in matching public expectations and the limitations of resources and infrastructure as well as political expediency, the Indian bureaucrat or '*babu*' has served the country's interests well and will continue to do so.

Ashwini Shrivastava, with his years of experience in observing the '*babudom*' from close quarters, will certainly throw more light on whether this steel framework of India's administration has been able to live up to the expectations of the country's citizens and if not, what is the way forward.

Such analysis from a generalist point of view, as he calls himself, will be profoundly useful because it provides an honest and unbiased feedback to the policy makers as well as the policy implementers for further improvement and to chalk out a road map for the future.

Sailaja Ray Baruah
Indian Revenue Service (IRS)/1987 Batch
Director General, Directorate General of Systems, Delhi

Functioning of bureaucracy

During the service years, one doesn't get time to write a book on the goings on in the bureaucracy, pleasant or otherwise.

Constraints in the form of seeking permissions and not stepping on someone's toes also prevent such a pleasurable activity as writing about the service which we love and which we have seen up close and personal.

Thus, some among the fraternity write about the anecdotes connected with their career after they hang up their boots and in their sunset years, before memory fades.

Ashwini Shrivastava, the author of this book on bureaucracy, suffers from no such constraints or inhibitions as he is a journalist by career and considers his job a mission to inform and do good to the society.

Although I have not had the opportunity to read the book itself, but from the conversation I had with him, I gather that this book is an outsider's look at how the bureaucracy works in this mighty land of ours.

He has carefully collated a lot of information which would be of interest to the aficionado of public administration and the general reader alike.

Ashwini is considered the 'bureaucrat's boy' in Delhi's administrative corridors and is one of the credible voices reporting on bureaucracy and governance related matters.

There is no gainsaying the fact that the administration at many levels suffers from some serious ailments.

Some of these are legacy issues, leftover from years of political and other interferences in the smooth functioning of the country.

However, many of them are defects which can, with some effort, be identified, diagnosed and even cured.

If the carrot does not work, the stick certainly will.

I gather that Ashwini has identified some of these systemic defects that have crept into the system and hampered the smooth flow of services to the common man.

As a seasoned journalist of many years with a keen eye for detail, he has penned his maiden work after years of observing the working of the system.

Aside from enumerating the faultlines, he has also suggested possible solutions in the bonus chapter appropriately titled as the '15 sutras for good governance', for ensuring sustainable good governance.

He assures me that these are not quick fire solutions or placebos but they are do-able.

I wish Ashwini all the luck in his maiden venture into book publishing and hope the book will be well received by the readers and at the news stands.

Dharmendra Kumar
IPS/1984 Batch/AGMUT cadre
Former Director General, Railway Protection Force (RPF)

On babus and babudom

For a diehard bureaucrat like me, one who is entering the thirty sixth year of service, writing a few lines on *Decoding Indian Babudom* has set me thinking on how we are perceived at present.

Are we so complex that we need to be decoded? Are we *Babus*, and do we make *Babudom*, a term in which *Babus* appear to be kings.

The fact is that we are changing, nay, transforming ourselves. However, shedding the baggage of centuries in a few years is not an easy task.

Our processes have indeed become more transparent, and the message from the PM is quite clear: Focus on Ease of Living and Ease of Doing Business.

I am not comfortable with the descriptor *Babu* for the bureaucracy – for our self image is quite different.

We think we are governance professionals, and we are committed to carrying out the constitutional mandate of creating an India that is inclusive, integrated and united. We look at everything not from a narrow sectorial perspective, but from a holistic viewpoint, which is so very important for field administrators, as well as for inputs into policy making for a country which is as diverse as ours.

We are not domain specialists, but we bring specialization of the context, for no intervention can be in a vacuum, and we are the ones who understand the eco-system of governance at the union, state, district and sub district levels far better than anyone else.

Sanjeev Chopra
IAS/1985 Batch/West Bengal cadre
Ex-Director, Lal Bahadur Shastri National Academy of Administration (LBSNAA), Mussoorie, Uttarakhand

Political pressure and bureaucracy

Bureaucracy has lost its intellectual rigour inspite of the high qualifications of the recruits because of the political pressures which are natural in a party based democracy.

Demands of the public are also complex. So, there is no point in following old procedures. At the same time, bureaucracy is now answerable to the Parliament and the Assemblies.

All this requires great skill not only for the bureaucrats, but also for the not-so-skilled elected representatives.

This may result in some conflict and conflict resolution is necessary. All this may result in delay or haphazard work. So training of the bureaucracy in modern skills has to be periodic and, at the same time, for the elected representatives too.

Dr G Sundaram
IAS/1962 Batch/Gujarat cadre
Former Secretary, Government of India

Digitization and good governance

Transparency is one of the major pre-requisites of good governance. Access to information (through the Right to Information Act and other means) not only ensures accountability, but also informs people about the good policy initiatives of the government for the marginalized sections of the society.

In a democracy, the government is supposed to act like a servant to the people and not the master but when it comes to application we see just the opposite.

We see that people find it difficult to get redressal for their grievances though it is the primary responsibility of the state.

It is the duty of the government to serve the people. It seems that the people are more disempowered than empowered. So, to change this, exercise of the voting right should not become a one day ritual.

A 2013 Supreme Court judgement, on the petition of T Subramaniam, says that the bureaucrats must be free from political influence. They should act on the written instructions of the political masters and filter them legally.

Further, the judgement says that transfer and posting of the officers must be on the basis of merit to deliver good governance. One can see how the essence of this judgement is flouted brazenly by the governments.

E-governance emphasizes digitization to promote good governance. Its absence or slow pace erodes people's trust in the government. Urgent steps must be taken towards ensuring 100 per cent digitization of all work related to public service delivery.

I am glad that Ashwini has mentioned the real ailments of the bureaucracy, especially the ones affecting the common people, and their possible solutions in a nutshell.

The contents of the book are easy to grasp. He has mentioned complex problems of the bureaucracy in simple words, thus helping the common people and large part of the government bureaucracy in understanding these challenges.

I find Ashwini's book unique as it talks about the problems faced by the people, especially those in rural areas, who are often neglected or considered unimportant by many.

Ashwini Shrivastava is a very well known name in the corridors of power from the central ministries to the headquarters of the states of Central India. He is a unique combination of journalistic acumen which ranges from transparency, governance and wild life issues.

He is an experienced journalist and this is reflected in his depiction of the *'babudom'* in this book.

I am sure governments and government employees (be it those under the central government or those working with the states) will go through this wonderful piece of work and try to bring some change that we all could see.

Ajay Dubey

Environmentalist and Social Activist

New age challenges

Governance is now technology driven and those who do not adopt it, will gradually fade away. The 'Steel frame of India' has to be cautious about not losing the human interface while managing the manifold dynamics of governance in a technology driven era.

There is a perpetual race among civil servants and legislators, to show the people who actually run the districts.

The general perception is that the District Collectors (DC) are the virtual government, but the Chief Minister of the respective state is the real boss, who checks accountability every day.

Social sector schemes like quality primary health, education, disaster management, maintenance of land records, redressal of public grievances, ground water management, crime control, timely payment of salaries to contractual labour and pension to the poor, among others, have not done well and are falling short of the Millennium Development Goals (MDGs).

Undoubtedly, the tools of governance have to be transformed to face the new age challenges of India.

There is already a churning: the question is should governance, especially of the economic ministries, be partly handed over to human resource on a lateral entry basis. The experiment is on and the results are yet to come in.

Most of the young brigade of civil servants and legislators are bright and result oriented but obtaining results still takes time.

There appears to be no magic wand unless the system is well oiled and put into automation mode. Why does a 'file' still take minimum 90 days to see the light of a final decision, irrespective of the pain pointed out by the Hon'ble Prime Minister?

Though the government has ordered the removal of non-performing baggage from the system, the speed of implementing this daring policy is still measured.

The adaptation of different management training modules of reputed foreign universities has been tested in the last decade and a huge sum has been spent by the Department of Personnel and Training (DoPT) from the tax payers' money but there is not a single research paper published on the impact on ground zero of the so-called transforming training programmes.

It's not the bureaucracy, but the government which drives the growth engine of India. The dispensation has to evolve a mechanism keeping in mind the needs of the soil rather than the influence of forces that be. Any mismatch between the need of the people and growth of the nation may lead to different complications in the future.

Ashwini Shrivastava's book *Decoding Indian Babudom* is a good initiative. It's a non-bureaucratic perception about governance, and an unconventional approach to deal with the subject.

Journalists have their own ways of analyzing the government and its workings. The 15 sutras like 'Proper implementation of transfer policies', 'Swachh (or clean) administration', 'Hundred per cent digitization of work' and 'Encourage innovations in governance', among others, suggested by Ashwini is a way forward for better governance.

He has highlighted both the problems and their solutions.

Ashwini Shrivastava's book is a wonderful addition to the literature of civil services of India and that too from a journalist's perspective.

Anil Tyagi
Editor
Gfiles (Magazine on civil services and governance)

Acknowledgements

I wish to express a deep sense of gratitude towards my parents – Mr Suresh Prasad Shrivastava and Mrs Sheela Shrivastava, my parents-in-law Dr Binod Shankar Singh and Mrs Seema Singh for their continuous support and encouragement in all my endeavours. Their blessings and guidance have made this writing possible.

No words could match the support I got from my wife Sumedha Shankar while penning down this book. Being a journalist herself, she also burned the midnight oil with me in helping to shape this volume.

I am indebted to R Chandrasekhar, my former colleague at the Press Trust of India (PTI), whose ever encouraging words kept me motivated to finish this book on time.

I am thankful to all my family members, friends, colleagues and civil servants for making this book possible.

I also wish to put on record the support from the publisher in ensuring timely publishing of the book despite the challenges thrown by COVID-19 pandemic.

मैं अकेला ही चला था जानिब-ए-मंज़िल मगर
लोग साथ आते गए और कारवाँ बनता गया

— मजरूहसुल्तानपुरी

'Micchāmi Dukkadam' is an ancient Indian phrase from Prakrit language. It is said to mean 'may all the evil that has been done be fruitless'. It is widely used to seek forgiveness.

I, unconditionally tender apology to all those who may have been hurt by my writing. I have penned this book to highlight some of the real ailments, in a few words, of the country's administrative system.

The aim of this book is to ensure that the governance of the country improves, especially for the downtrodden, neglected and marginalized people.

I have a submission to make: I was repeatedly asked to include some of the controversial bureaucratic instances in this book to help it sell. However, I rejected it primarily for the fact that I don't want those cases to overshadow the ailments of bureaucracy.

I am willing to come out with a second edition of the book carrying a separate chapter mentioning some of the stories behind the most-talked about bureaucratic incidents of the time, provided readers demand that.

Many thanks for finding time to go through this.

About the Author

Ashwini has been practising journalism for over 15 years. He is considered a credible resource person on India's governance, bureaucracy, anti-corruption and on the Right to Information (RTI) Act related subjects, among others.

Ashwini is one of the few active journalists in the country who regularly exercises his right to know, to get governance related details from different central government departments. He has done a number of stories on the basis of information obtained through these RTI applications. So far, he has filed over 500 applications under the RTI Act.

Many of his stories, done on the basis of information obtained from RTI queries, have been raised in the Indian Parliament too.

Ashwini has travelled widely, abroad and within the country, with VVIPs including former Presidents and Vice Presidents of India. He has been doing regular programmes on All India Radio (AIR) – India's national broadcaster, on contemporary issues.

He is an alumnus of the US-based East West Centre and

Asia Journalism Fellowship (AJF) organized by the Institute of Policy Studies under the National University of Singapore (NUS), Singapore.

Ashwini was guest speaker at the 'Global Inequalities and Extremism' conference during Global Media Forum organized by Deutsche Welle in 2018 at Bonn in Germany.

He has attended several national and international workshops and webinars prominent among them are the ones on peace journalism, visual news gathering and environmental journalism organized by the US-based East West Centre.

An avid traveler with a penchant for wildlife, Ashwini holds Master of Journalism and Communication (MJC), Post Graduate Diploma in Print and Electronic Media, Bachelor of Journalism and Communication (BJC) and Bachelor of Computer Applications (BCA) degrees besides the 'Religion, Conflict and Peace' course by Harvard University, USA.

Currently, he is working as Assistant Editor with the Press Trust of India – the country's largest news agency – at its headquarters in Delhi.

He can be contacted at ashwinishrivastava@gmail.com and followed at Twitter: @ashwinijourno